SPIRIT
WRESTLER

SPIRIT WRESTLER

GREG NELSON

COTEAU BOOKS

© Greg Nelson, 1998.

All rights reserved. No part of this book covered by the copyrights hereon may be reproduced or used in any form or by any means—graphic, electronic or mechanical—without the prior written permission of the publisher. Any request for photocopying, recording, taping, or storage in information storage and retrieval systems of any part of this book shall be directed in writing to CanCopy, 6 Adelaide Street East, Suite 900, Toronto, Ontario, M5C 1H6.

Spirit Wrestler is a work of fiction. Although many of the characters and scenes are based on actual figures and events, no attempt has been made to be historically accurate. Huge liberties have been taken throughout.

Photos on page 110-111, courtesy Twenty Fifth Street Theatre, Saskatoon, Saskatchewan. Act I and II frontispiece photos, and photos on page 55 (except Tolstoy photo), 58, and 109, courtesy Provincial Archives of British Columbia. Photo of Leo Tolstoy on page 55, courtesy Saskatchewan Archives Board.

Cover design by Ed Pas.
Cover image, *The Burning of the Arms*, by Terry McLean, photo by Bill McKeowan. From the collection of Larry Ewashen. Reproduced with permission.
Book design by Duncan Campbell.
Printed and bound in Canada.

Coteau Books acknowledges the financial support of: the Government of Canada through the Canada Council for the Arts; the Department of Canadian Heritage Book Publishing Industry Development Program and Multiculturalism Programs; the Government of Saskatchewan through the Saskatchewan Arts Board; and the City of Regina through the Regina Arts Commission, for our publishing activities.

Coteau Books celebrates the 50ᵀᴴ Anniversary of the Saskatchewan Arts Board, and the 40ᵀᴴ Anniversary of the Canada Council for the Arts with this publication.

Canadian Cataloguing in Publication Data

Nelson, Greg, 1965-
Spirit wrestler
A play.
ISBN 1-55050-126-7

1. Doukhobors—Canada—Drama. 1. Title.
PS8577.E354 S75 1998   C812'.54   C98-920016-7
PR9199.3.N45 S75 1998

COTEAU BOOKS
401-2206 Dewdney Avenue
Regina, Saskatchewan
CANADA   S4R 1H3

AVAILABLE IN THE U.S. FROM:

GENERAL DISTRIBUTION SERVICES
85 River Rock Road, Suite 202
Buffalo, New York
USA   14207

To Patti

PLAYWRIGHT'S NOTE

Spirit Wrestler began in the fall of 1991 when I met George Stushnoff, Chairman of the Doukhobor Society of Saskatchewan. He was planning the 1995 celebrations of the 100TH anniversary of The Burning of Arms, and wanted someone to write a play. I expressed interest, funding was obtained from Canada Council's Explorations program, and the project was underway.

Throughout 1992, I immersed myself in Doukhobor history. I read everything I could find, visited Verigin, Saskatchewan and the Grand Forks/Castlegar region in British Columbia, conducted research at the University of Saskatchewan and University of British Columbia special collections, and spoke to many Doukhobors. And then I began the difficult process of getting rid of all that research, and clearing enough space in my head to write the play.

I discovered very early in the writing that, although I was not a Doukhobor, their history and faith had directly to do with me. I became interested in what their story revealed about Canadian history and consciousness. I was caught by the exhilaration of their faith.

I want to emphasize that *Spirit Wrestler* is a work of fiction. Although many of the characters and scenes are based on actual figures and events, no attempt whatsoever has been made to be historically accurate. Huge liberties have been taken throughout.

ACKNOWLEDGEMENTS

Spirit Wrestler would not have been written, produced, or published without the funding of the Canada Council for the Arts and the Saskatchewan Arts Board. Also vital to the process was the Saskatchewan Playwrights Centre, who provided two workshops. Some of the research was done at the Wallace Stegner House in Eastend, Saskatchewan. Final rewrites were done at the Sage Hill Writing Experience.

Two of the many Doukhobors who assisted in the research are Larry Ewashen and George Stushnoff.

My thanks to the following people, who provided support and encouragement: George Stushnoff, Jim DeFelice, John Murrell, Vern Thiessen, Tom Bentley-Fisher, and Patti Shedden.

—*Greg Nelson*

PREMIERE PRODUCTION

Spirit Wrestler premièred at Twenty-Fifth Street Theatre, Saskatoon, on October 27, 1995, with the following cast:

LEBEDEV / VASILY / ZIBAROFF	*Kent Allen*
SAVELY/ VERIGIN	*Kelly Handerek*
NIKOLAI	*Tom Rooney*
ANNA	*Sharon Bakker*
NAKASHIDZE / MCDOUGALL	*Frederick Edell*
GUBANOFF / MAVOR	*Rod MacIntyre*
ZUBKOFF / SIFTON	*Kristian Marken*
TANYA	*Patricia Drake*

DIRECTED BY *Tom Bentley-Fisher*
SET AND LIGHTING DESIGN BY *Colin Ross*
COSTUME DESIGN BY *Theresa Germain*
STAGE MANAGED BY *Angus Ferguson*

The production also featured the Saskatoon Doukhobor Choral Group:

Ryan Androsoff, Virginia Androsoff, Ella Boke, Shirley Brylinski, Jeanette Derksen, Lucille Dergousoff, Michael Dergousoff, Delphine Fedosoff, Ivan Fedosoff, Marian Kalesnikoff, Bill Kalmakoff, June Kalmakoff, Shelley Lavertu, John Meakin, Violet Nemanishen, Annette Popoff, Mae Popoff, Vera Popoff, John Papove, Kay Papove, Elsie Perehudoff, Kathleen Rezansoff, Bill Strelioff, George Stushnoff, Verna Thompson, Polly Tokaryk, Edna Wright.

Spirit Wrestler was given a three-day workshop in May 1994 at the Saskatchewan Playwrights Centre's Spring Festival of New Plays, in Regina. It was directed by Tom Bentley-Fisher and dramaturged by Patti Shedden. Workshop actors were:

Vern Thiessen, Burgandy Code, Kent Allen, Pamela Haig-Bartley, Kelly Handerek, Dwayne Brenna, Rob Roy, and Brad Grass.

CHARACTERS

NIKOLAI	*A Doukhobor man. Ages 14-30.*
ANNA	*Anna Kalmakoff. Nikolai's Mother.*
SAVELY	*Savely Kalmakoff. Nikolai's Father.*
TANYA	*Tanya Petrovna Popoff. Nikolai's age.*
LEBEDEV	*A Doukhobor man in his twenties.*
GUBANOFF	*Michael Gubanoff. A Doukhobor leader.*
ZUBKOFF	*Alyosha Zubkoff. A Doukhobor leader.*
NAKASHIDZE	*Governor of Caucasus Region, Russia.*
VASILY	*Vasily Verigin. Peter Verigin's brother.*
MAVOR	*James Mavor. Professor, University of Toronto. Scottish accent.*
SIFTON	*Clifford Sifton. Minister of the Interior. English accent.*
ZIBAROFF	*A radical Doukhobor.*
VERIGIN	*Peter Verigin. Doukhobor Leader 1886-1924.*
MCDOUGALL	*John McDougall. A civil servant.*

CASTING BREAKDOWN: 2 WOMEN, 6 MEN

NIKOLAI	NAKASHIDZE/MCDOUGALL
SAVELY/VERIGIN	ZUBKOFF/SIFTON
ANNA	GUBANOFF/ZIBAROFF
TANYA	LEBEDEV/VASILY/MAVOR

SETTING

ACT ONE: *Russia, approximately 1895.*
ACT TWO: *Canada, approximately 1908.*

NOTE ON PUNCTUATION

The punctuation of *Spirit Wrestler* ignores the rules of grammar in favour of the rhythms of speech. This is a deliberate choice. Periods, commas, ellipses, and question marks are used to indicate rhythm and inflection—how the lines should be delivered by the actor.

An ellipsis (...) at the end of speech indicates a trailing off. An em dash (—) indicates an interruption by the following speech.

Peter Verigin

ACT ONE

Act One—Scene One

A Doukhobor Choir sings in the dark. Lights come up on a group of Doukhobor men, including NIKOLAI, *working silently in a field. He is 14. They work as the singing fades. Eventually, one of the men speaks as he works.*

LEBEDEV: This morning, on my way to this field, I met a man on the road. And the man said to me: "Who are you?" "My name?" I said. "My name is Matvey. Matvey Lebedev." And the man said: "Do you believe in God?" And I said, "Yes, of course I believe in God: I am a Doukhobor." "A Doukhobor?" "Yes," I said. "And what does that mean?" The man said: "What does that mean?"

The other men ignore the speaker. Except for NIKOLAI, *who stops working, and looks at him.*

And so I told him. I told him that I live in peace. That I believe that killing is wrong. Bloodshed is wrong. I believe my body is a temple, of God, that God is living inside me, as He does in every living thing, and so it follows if I harm another living thing, then I am therefore harming God. And then the man said, "Yes, but Matvey...surely, you are corrupt. Surely you are living in sin. Are you not prosperous? Do you not have wealth, and worldly goods? Do you not slaughter animals, and eat them? Do you not corrupt your body with alcohol and smoke? Do you not own weapons? Have you not abandoned the ways of your fathers?"

And astonished, I looked at this man. And he looked back at me. I felt his eyes upon me, looking into me, inside me. And I found that I could not return his gaze. And as I cast my eyes upon the road, I asked him: "Brother, who are *you?* What is *your* name?" And he told me. "Verigin." He said: "My name...is Peter Verigin."

The other men have left, or moved away. NIKOLAI *stands, looking at the Doukhobor man, who continues working.* SAVELY'S *voice is heard from offstage.*

Scene Two

SAVELY: *(Off, calling.)* Nikolai?

NIKOLAI *doesn't move. He stands still, staring at the man.*

(Calling.) Nikolai?

NIKOLAI *starts. The man exits.* NIKOLAI *sits on a stool, opens a book.*

Nikolai, come here.

NIKOLAI *ignores* SAVELY, *reads.*

(Sharp.) Nikolai!

NIKOLAI: I'm in here!

NIKOLAI *hides the book.* SAVELY *enters, with a cane, limping. He is drunk.*

SAVELY: I was calling you.

NIKOLAI *ignores him.*

Why should I have to get up? Eh? I'm the one with this leg, not you.

NIKOLAI: I'm sorry.

SAVELY: No you're not. If you were sorry you'd have some consideration.

NIKOLAI: I—

SAVELY: But you don't.

NIKOLAI: I said—

SAVELY: You should come to me.

NIKOLAI: I said I was sorry.

SAVELY: Come here. I'm your father, I'm not going to eat you.

NIKOLAI *doesn't move.*

Nikolai. Come here.

NIKOLAI *still doesn't move.* **SAVELY** *takes out his pipe, fills it with tobacco, lights it.*

Did you finish your chores?

NIKOLAI: Yes.

SAVELY: All of them?

NIKOLAI: Yes.

SAVELY: What were you doing in here. When I called.

NIKOLAI: Nothing.

SAVELY: Were you reading?

NIKOLAI: No.

SAVELY: Reading books? Eh?

NIKOLAI: *No.*

Pause. **SAVELY** *smokes.*

SAVELY: Guess who I spoke with today. Eli Grigorovitch. Do you know what I asked him? "Eli," I said to him, "Eli—tell me about my son." "Your son?" says Eli. "Yes," I say, "My Nikolai. Tell me: Is he a good worker? Does he pull his weight? In the fields?" And do you know what he says to me? "Well Savely," he says, "he's a good boy." "I know he's a good *boy*, Eli," I say to him, "I know he's a good *boy*, I'm asking, is he a good *worker.*" And you know what he says?

"Well," he says, "Well, Savely," he says..."He's a dreamer. Your Nikolai. He's a little bit...of a dreamer." *(Slight pause. Looking at* NIKOLAI:*)* Eli Grigorovitch.

SAVELY *smokes. Pause. During the following,* ANNA *enters, watches.*

I wish that I could have been there, Nikolai. Today, in the fields. Working in the sun. I would have been happy. I wouldn't have cared about anything. I would have felt my muscles, moving under my shirt, the sweat beginning to run. My leg, working. I would have heard the voice of God, telling me that what I was doing was good. That I was doing good.

"By the sweat of your face you shall eat bread until you return to the ground. For out of the ground you were taken. You are dust, and to dust you shall return."

Listen to your father. This is good advice. Don't worry about this. *(Pokes his head.)* Don't fill it up with books, they aren't your concern. *(Holds up his hands.)* These are your concerns. The land. The soil. Look at my hands. Look! What do you see there, in the creases.

NIKOLAI: Soil, father.

SAVELY: *Soil.* The soil is a part of my hand, Nikolai. I can't wash it out, it's a part of me, a part of my body. Be true to the soil. For if you are true to the soil, you are true to yourself. Understand? You are true to God.

NIKOLAI: I don't believe you.

SAVELY: Eh?

NIKOLAI: You didn't speak to Eli Grigorovitch. Because he won't be seen with you any more. He's embarrassed by you. He finds you embarrassing.

ANNA: Nikolai.

NIKOLAI: Do you know what they say about you in the village?

ANNA: What are you doing.

NIKOLAI: They say you're lazy. Your leg is just an excuse. They call you a drunk.

SAVELY: Who are you talking to?

NIKOLAI: It's time for you to stop. Stop drinking, stop smoking, and stop eating meat. You have become corrupt. You have abandoned the ways of your fathers. You're not serving God any longer. You're serving yourself.

SAVELY: Who do you think—

NIKOLAI: (*Suddenly loud.*) You. I'm talking to *you!*

Sudden pause. SAVELY *looks at* NIKOLAI *for a moment, then turns to* ANNA.

SAVELY: This is your fault.

ANNA: Savely—

SAVELY: This is what comes of his books.

ANNA: Don't be ridiculous.

SAVELY: (*Mounting fury.*) What have you been telling him?

ANNA: I haven't—

SAVELY: You've been filling his head with garbage! This is how he talks to his father? This is the respect he shows to his father? What have you been telling him?

NIKOLAI: (*Yelling overtop of him.*) You're disgusting! You're a disgrace! All you do is sit around and drink!

SAVELY *is about to hit* NIKOLAI.

ANNA: Savely, no!

SAVELY *hits him.* NIKOLAI *flinches, but doesn't back down.*

DON'T HIT HIM!

Pause. Then SAVELY *slumps.*

SAVELY: Please. Nikolai. Just...do your work. Promise me. Please. Promise me you'll do your work. Nikolai? Promise me.

NIKOLAI *says nothing.* SAVELY *gets up.*

If I find any books, I will burn them.

He begins to leave.

NIKOLAI: What about the Bible? Will you burn that?

SAVELY: *(Stopping, turning.)* Our Bible is in here, Nikolai. *(Points to his chest.)* Our Living Book. Beware of words on paper. They are written by men. Not by God.

SAVELY *exits.* NIKOLAI *watches him go.*

ANNA: He's a fool. Come here, Nikolai. *(*NIKOLAI *doesn't.)* Nikki.

NIKOLAI *doesn't move.*

Your father is wicked. He's corrupt. When we are in Paradise, he will be consumed by fire.

NIKOLAI *looks at her. Slight pause.*

Do you know what I heard today in the village? A woman was blind, and Peter Verigin healed her. He made her see. Another man was lame, and now he can walk. An old man said that, on the night that Peter was born, he saw a star falling on the Verigin house. A star from the heavens, Nikolai.

She moves to him. She runs her hand through his hair.

I can feel it. Inside me. The Living Christ has come.

Scene Three

NAKASHIDZE's *Office*. NAKASHIDZE, GUBANOFF, ZUBKOFF.

NAKASHIDZE: Peter Verigin.

GUBANOFF: Yes. Governor, he's a fanatic.

ZUBKOFF: He's an impostor.

GUBANOFF: A very dangerous man.

ZUBKOFF: Entire villages have fallen under his spell.

GUBANOFF: Hundreds of Doukhobors.

ZUBKOFF: Possibly thousands.

GUBANOFF: We thought you should know.

ZUBKOFF: You see, we're not sure what he's capable of.

GUBANOFF: Violence certainly.

ZUBKOFF: Possibly insurrection.

GUBANOFF: He's out of control.

ZUBKOFF: He really should be exiled.

GUBANOFF: That's right: exiled. To Siberia.

ZUBKOFF: And his followers should be neutralized.

GUBANOFF: That's right.

ZUBKOFF: And his teachings made illegal.

GUBANOFF: We're confident you'll see the danger here—

ZUBKOFF: —and act accordingly.

GUBANOFF: For which, of course, we would be most grateful.

ZUBKOFF: You see, as of now we possess the Orphan's Home—

GUBANOFF: —our treasury—

ZUBKOFF: —and, with your assistance, Governor—

GUBANOFF: —we will continue—

ZUBKOFF: —to possess it.

NAKASHIDZE: Drink?

GUBANOFF: I'm sorry?

NAKASHIDZE has been pouring vodkas as they talked. Now he holds glasses out to them.

NAKASHIDZE: Would you like a vodka.

GUBANOFF: *(Slight pause.)* Yes.

ZUBKOFF: Thank you.

They each take a vodka.

NAKASHIDZE: *(Toasting.)* The Tsar.

ZUBKOFF & GUBANOFF: *(In Unison.)* Our Saviour Jesus Christ.

They drink. NAKASHIDZE *regards them.*

NAKASHIDZE: Well, I must say this is a surprise. A delegation of Doukhobors. Here in my office. It's quite an occasion.

ZUBKOFF: Well, we thought you should know.

GUBANOFF: About Verigin.

ZUBKOFF: The danger.

GUBANOFF: We knew you would want to take....To take....

ZUBKOFF: Action.

NAKASHIDZE *says nothing. He looks at them. Pause.*

NAKASHIDZE: You know, I've always admired you. Doukhobors. I've admired your strength, your...faith. Your refusal to compromise.

He pauses.

Now, correct me if I'm wrong. You Doukhobors are pacifists, yes?

GUBANOFF: Yes.

NAKASHIDZE: You refuse to be conscripted. You refuse to fight.

GUBANOFF: That's right.

NAKASHIDZE: You refuse to pledge allegiance to the Tsar.

GUBANOFF: We—

NAKASHIDZE: *(Not stopping.)* Saying that, as Christians, your allegiance is to God, and God alone. Yes?

GUBANOFF: Well—

NAKASHIDZE: You refuse, in point of fact, to have anything to do with the Tsar. Or his armies. Or his government. Or his laws. Yes?

GUBANOFF: Governor—

NAKASHIDZE: Please. I just want to be clear.

Slight pause. GUBANOFF *looks to* ZUBKOFF.

ZUBKOFF: *(Wary.)* Yes.

NAKASHIDZE: Yes. And this is what you *believe*. Isn't that interesting. Really. I find it fascinating. This is what you believe, so therefore, this is what you do. Wonderful. *(Slight pause.)* It must be very difficult for you. To come here, as you have done today, to come before the Tsar's Governor, and beg.

ZUBKOFF: Well—

NAKASHIDZE: To act so blatantly against your beliefs. Yes? It must be very hard.

ZUBKOFF: We're not exactly begging, Governor.

GUBANOFF: We're providing you with information.

ZUBKOFF: Valuable information.

GUBANOFF: That's right.

ZUBKOFF: We're helping you to keep the peace.

NAKASHIDZE: I am capable of keeping the peace. *(Pause.)* Gentlemen, please. Let's be absolutely clear. This Verigin is not a threat to me. He is a threat to you. Hm? And that is why you are here.

He pauses.

> Tell me something. Would you agree that there exists, between a ruler and his people, a...a contract, an exchange. The one provides the other with certain things, say for example taxes, and is provided, in return, with other things: protection, government, order, so on. Yes?

ZUBKOFF: Well—

NAKASHIDZE: *(Interrupting.)* Yes or no.

Slight pause. ZUBKOFF *nods, wary.*

Yes. Now. Would you agree that the Tsar, in his wisdom, and, indeed, his generosity, has, of late, allowed you Doukhobors to *opt out* of this contract? He has made of your people an exception. A special case. Perhaps because, as I do, he respects the fact that you have beliefs, he admires you. Yes?

ZUBKOFF *nods.*

Yes. Good. Good. Now. Would you agree...that by coming here today, by asking me to: *(Itemizing on his fingers.)* exile this Verigin, neutralize his followers, and outlaw his teachings, you are, in effect, asking to be let back in? Yes? To this contract?

ZUBKOFF: Governor, please, we have money—

GUBANOFF: Plenty of money—

ZUBKOFF: You'd be acting in your own best interests—

NAKASHIDZE: *(Interrupting.)* Answer the question. Would you agree?

ZUBKOFF: *(Pause.)* Yes.

NAKASHIDZE: You would. Excellent. Thank you. That's very clear. Good.

He smiles at them.

All right. Yes, I will exile Peter Verigin. I will make his teachings illegal. I will remove the threat.

ZUBKOFF: *(Relief.)* Thank you, Governor.

GUBANOFF: You are very kind.

ZUBKOFF: You won't regret this, I promise—

NAKASHIDZE: I'm not finished.

They look at him. Slight pause.

> I will do these things. And in return...you will provide me with soldiers. For my battalions.

GUBANOFF: Soldiers?

NAKASHIDZE: Further, you will ensure that each and every Doukhobor man, woman, and child swears an oath of allegiance. To the Tsar.

GUBANOFF: But Governor—

NAKASHIDZE: Those are my terms.

GUBANOFF *looks in panic to* ZUBKOFF.

GUBANOFF: Governor, please. I don't think you understand. What you are asking is beyond our power to grant, we, we, we simply—

ZUBKOFF: We accept.

GUBANOFF: What?

ZUBKOFF: *(To* NAKASHIDZE.*)* We accept your terms.

GUBANOFF: We do? No we don't.

ZUBKOFF: Yes, Michael, we do.

GUBANOFF *and* ZUBKOFF *look at each other, in silent struggle.* NAKASHIDZE *watches, keenly.* ZUBKOFF *wins the struggle.*

NAKASHIDZE: Interesting. I didn't think you would. I must say: I'm rather disappointed. However.

He pours vodkas, hands them around.

> The Tsar.

ACT ONE—13

ZUBKOFF: *(Raises glass.)* The Tsar.

They look at GUBANOFF.

GUBANOFF: *(Pauses, then raises glass.)* The Tsar.

Scene Four

The fields. NIKOLAI *speaks to a group of Doukhobors, who stand, facing him, listening.*

NIKOLAI: I met a man today on the road. Do you know what he told me? He said we cannot serve two masters. He said our allegiance is to God, and God alone. He said we have been betrayed. Bought and sold. We have all been sent into exile. Our leaders have sent our faith, our very souls into exile. They have made us into murderers. Soldiers and murderers. This is what the man said. He said we must say No. He said we must resist.

Scene Five

ANNA'S *kitchen.* ANNA *is working, humming to herself.* VASILY *stands in the doorway, watching her. She senses his presence, turns.)*

ANNA: *(Startled.)* Oh.

VASILY: I'm sorry. Did I startle you?

ANNA: Yes.

VASILY: Forgive me. May I come in?

ANNA: My husband's not here.

VASILY: Yes—

ANNA: He's in the village—

VASILY: I know where he is. I don't want to speak with him. I want to speak with you.

ANNA: With me?

VASILY: And with your son. My name is Vasily Verigin.

ANNA: Verigin?

VASILY: Yes. As in brother of Peter.

ANNA: Oh. Oh I see.

ANNA, *stunned, doesn't know what to do.*

VASILY: May I come in?

ANNA: Yes of course. I'm sorry. Please.

VASILY: Thank you.

ANNA: Please come in.

VASILY: *(Bowing.)* Peace be to this house.

ANNA: *(Bowing, responding quickly, a ritual response.)* With gladness we receive this peace, and with you joyfully praise it.

VASILY: God be praised.

ANNA: *(Overlapping.)* God be praised.

Another slightly stunned pause.

Please. Sit down.

VASILY: Thank you.

VASILY *sits.* ANNA, *standing, looks at him.*

ANNA: You are welcome here. In this house.

ACT ONE—15

VASILY: Thank you.

ANNA: Very welcome. I want you to know. We disagree with my husband. We think he's corrupt.

VASILY: Yes—

ANNA: And sinful.

VASILY: Yes, I know you do.

ANNA: You wanted to speak to my son? He's outside.

VASILY: Wait. Don't call him. Not yet. *(Gestures to a chair.)* Please.

ANNA *sits next to him. He pauses.*

> I'm not sure what you know about us, Anna, or how much you've heard. We've established contact with my brother, in Siberia. He has given us several...directives. Do you understand?

ANNA *nods, wide-eyed.*

> I'll come straight to the point. Your son's name has come up. We are hoping he will help us, with the young men. I have come to ask your blessing.

ANNA: You have it.

VASILY: Just a moment—

ANNA: *(Fierce.)* We support you, and your brother, completely. My son would do anything, and so would I—

VASILY: No—

ANNA: He is going to be a great man. A *leader*. Because he has faith. He *believes*.

VASILY: No, I'm sorry, I don't think you understand. I'm saying he might not live.

ANNA: What?

VASILY: I'm saying he might die. Your son. If you call him in here, if I speak to him tonight, it will very likely lead to his imprisonment and death.

Slight pause, VASILY *looking carefully at* ANNA.

Now, all you have to do is ask me to leave. I will turn and walk away and your son will never know I was here. But if you call him, he will be at risk. At terrible risk. Do you understand this now?

ANNA: Yes.

VASILY: Do you want me to leave?

Pause.

ANNA: We believe...

Pause.

We believe in Peter Verigin, that he will lead us to salvation. We do not believe in governments, or Tsars, but in God, in God, that God is dwelling within us, that....

VASILY: Anna.

ANNA: That our bodies are his temples, that....

VASILY: Do you want me to leave?

Pause.

ANNA: No.

VASILY: Thank you Anna. All right. You may call him.

ANNA *doesn't call him. Pause. Then, she calls him.*

ANNA: Nikolai.
No response.

Nikolai.

NIKOLAI: *(Off.)* What?

ANNA: Come in here please.

NIKOLAI: Why?

ANNA: There's somebody here. He wants to meet you.

NIKOLAI *enters.*

Nikolai. This man is Vasily Verigin.

NIKOLAI: Verigin?

ANNA: Yes. He's Peter Verigin's brother.

VASILY: Hello Nikolai.

ANNA: He wants to talk to you.

Slight pause. Then NIKOLAI *bows.*

NIKOLAI: *(Ritual greeting.)* May God bless you and give you peace.

VASILY: *(Bowing, ritual response.)* Blessings from the Heavenly Hosts.

ANNA: *(Rising, indicating her chair.)* Sit here.

NIKOLAI *looks at her.*

Go on.

NIKOLAI *sits.* ANNA *stands behind him.*

VASILY: I've just been speaking with your mother. She says you're going to be a great man, some day. A leader. Do you agree?

NIKOLAI: I just want to serve God.

VASILY: I see.

ANNA: *(Prompting Nikolai.)* God, and....

NIKOLAI: And Peter Verigin. God and Peter Verigin.

VASILY *looks at him for a moment. Then he launches into a catechism.*

VASILY: What kind of person are you?

NIKOLAI: *(Slight pause.)* I am a Doukhobor.

VASILY: Why are you called Doukhobor?

NIKOLAI: To glorify God.

VASILY: What does the Doukhobor cross represent?

NIKOLAI: A narrow path, a life of a pil—

ANNA: *(Interrupting, prompting.)* Sorrow.

NIKOLAI: A narrow path, voluntary sorrow, a life of a pilgrim, a life of poverty.

VASILY: To what law do you belong?

NIKOLAI: To God's law.

VASILY: What is God's law?

NIKOLAI: What I do not wish for myself, I do not wish for my brother.

VASILY: Where do you see God?

NIKOLAI: His sovereignty is everywhere.

VASILY: *(Slight pause.)* And Peter Verigin?

NIKOLAI: He is the Living Christ, our saviour. He will lead us, through suffering, to salvation.

VASILY: Through suffering.

NIKOLAI: Yes.

VASILY: What does that mean.

NIKOLAI: It—

VASILY: Do you know what that means?

NIKOLAI: Yes—

VASILY: Do you?

NIKOLAI *looks at him.*

> We keep hearing about you Nikolai. Your name keeps... popping up. Do you know why I'm here?

NIKOLAI *shakes his head.*

> We're hoping you might help us. Would you like to help us?

NIKOLAI *nods.*

> Can you read?

NIKOLAI *nods.*

> Good. This just arrived from Siberia.

He holds out a letter to NIKOLAI. NIKOLAI, *awestruck, hesitates.*

> Go ahead, you may take it.

NIKOLAI *takes it.*

The Tsar is demanding an oath, from all of his subjects, an oath of allegiance. My brother has refused this oath.

They flogged him. Still he refused, saying: "No man can serve two masters." *(Slight pause.)* These are his instructions. No Doukhobor is to take the oath of allegiance. No Doukhobor is to pay any taxes. And finally, no Doukhobor is to engage in military service. Period. Those already engaged are to put down their guns. Whatever the consequence.

NIKOLAI: They'll be beaten.

VASILY: Yes.

NIKOLAI: They might even be killed.

VASILY: Yes, Nikolai, that's right. They might. *(Pointing at the letter.)* Read this please. From here.

NIKOLAI *reads.* ANNA *watches him. After a moment,* NIKOLAI *looks up.*

NIKOLAI: When will this happen?

VASILY: June 29th. St. Peter's Day. Do you understand what it means? What it could lead to?

NIKOLAI: Yes.

VASILY: Do you still want to help us?

NIKOLAI *looks to* ANNA. *She nods.*

NIKOLAI: Yes.

VASILY: Good. The first thing we must do, is find the weapons. They exist in every Doukhobor house: knives, guns....We must find them. Quickly. And above all, secretly. Nobody must know what—

VASILY *breaks off.* SAVELY *is standing in the doorway.*

ANNA: Savely.

VASILY: Good evening.

ANNA: How long have you—

VASILY: *(Interrupting.)* Your wife has been extremely kind. I was in need of water, for my horse.

ANNA: *(Playing along)* That's right. This man has been travelling all day. I gave him some tea.

SAVELY *says nothing. He is drunk.*

VASILY: Well. I should be on my way. *(To* ANNA.*)* Thank you for the tea.

ANNA: Not at all. It was a pleasure making your acquaintance.

VASILY: Yes—

ANNA: Please come again some time.

VASILY: *(Moving to door.)* Thank you. Good night.

ANNA: Good night.

NIKOLAI: *(For* VASILY'*s benefit.)* Have you been drinking father?

VASILY, *at the door, stops, turns.*

(To SAVELY.*)* Your breath stinks. Of alcohol. And meat.

SAVELY: None of your business.

NIKOLAI: It *is* my business, father. If you are sinning, that is my business.

SAVELY: You—

NIKOLAI: If you are not a true Doukhobor, that is my business!

Pause. SAVELY *looks at* NIKOLAI. *Then, he turns to* VASILY.

SAVELY: Listen to me. I am a good man. I have worked hard. All of my life. Do you understand me? Peter Verigin can go to the devil.

Pause. VASILY *looks at him, says nothing.*

NIKOLAI: We are leaving this house, father. From this moment on, you do not have a son.

ANNA: Or a wife.

NIKOLAI: We are Doukhobors, here.

Scene Six

The kitchen of TANYA'S *house.* TANYA *and* NIKOLAI. TANYA *has been polishing two silver candlesticks.* NIKOLAI *stands in the doorway.*

TANYA: Nikolai.

NIKOLAI: Good evening, I—

TANYA: Isn't that funny. I was just thinking about you.

NIKOLAI: What?

TANYA: And here you are.

NIKOLAI: I....You were?

TANYA: You can come in Nikolai. You don't have to lurk in the doorway.

NIKOLAI: I'm here to see your brother.

ACT ONE—23

TANYA: *(Slight pause.)* My brother?

NIKOLAI: Yes. It's business.

TANYA: What is.

NIKOLAI: With your brother. I've come on a matter of business.

TANYA: *(Slight pause.)* Well then. You'd better sit down.

TANYA *looks steadily at him.* NIKOLAI *blushes, sits.*

My brother's not home.

NIKOLAI: *(Getting up.)* Oh—

TANYA: Sit down.

NIKOLAI *sits.*

He'll be back in a minute. What kind of business.

NIKOLAI: I can't tell you. It's a secret.

She just looks at him.

I have instructions. From Peter Verigin.

TANYA: *You* do.

NIKOLAI: Yes.

TANYA: You've been talking to Peter Verigin.

NIKOLAI: No. To his brother.

TANYA: Oh his *brother.*

NIKOLAI: It's true! He came to my house and, and he gave me instructions, and....*(With dignity.)* And now I'm passing them on. To certain people. That's my job.

TANYA: Would you like some tea?

NIKOLAI: Yes. Thank you.

TANYA: Help yourself.

NIKOLAI *goes to the samovar, gets tea.* TANYA *watches his back.*

> We've been talking about you, Nikolai. My friends and I. They seem to like you for some reason.

NIKOLAI *turns, looks at her.*

> Sit down.

He sits.

> So what's the secret?

NIKOLAI: I can't tell you.

TANYA: Why not?

NIKOLAI: Because—

TANYA: Can you give me a hint?

NIKOLAI: No.

TANYA: Why did they pick you?

NIKOLAI: I don't know.

TANYA: Is it too hot?

NIKOLAI: What?

TANYA: The tea. Is it too hot.

NIKOLAI: Oh— *(He sips.)* No. It's good.

She watches him drink his tea for a moment.

TANYA: How's your father?

No response. He stares at his tea.

I heard he locked himself inside the house and won't come out.

NIKOLAI: I don't care what he does. He's got nothing to do with me.

TANYA: Where are you living?

NIKOLAI: With my aunt.

TANYA: Is that all right?

NIKOLAI: It's better than living with him.

TANYA: Really? *(Looking at him.)* Nikolai. Are you okay?

NIKOLAI: Yes.

TANYA: Are you?

NIKOLAI: Yes. *(Slight pause.)* Something has happened. A Doukhobor soldier has put down his gun. A soldier named Lebedev.

TANYA: Really.

NIKOLAI: Matvey Lebedev. He put down his gun and refused to pick it up.

TANYA: And what happened.

NIKOLAI: They threw him in jail. In a dark cell, they kicked him and beat him and beat him until he can't even stand. He lies on the floor in a pool of blood.

TANYA: Is that the secret?

NIKOLAI: No, the secret is what happens next. What we're going to do. That's all I'm saying.

TANYA: What are we going to do?

NIKOLAI: That's all I'm saying.

TANYA: Nikolai—

NIKOLAI: It will mean suffering. It might even mean death.

TANYA: What will.

NIKOLAI: We refuse the government! We refuse the Tsar! We accept only love and peace and God. And if we have to suffer, then we will, as *Christ* suffered, and through our suffering we will overcome the sins of the world!

TANYA: Very impressive.

NIKOLAI: What.

TANYA: You certainly know how to talk. Is that what you're going to say to my brother? He's going to love it. Tell me something, Nikolai. If Peter Verigin walked into this kitchen right now and told you to shoot yourself in the head, with a gun, would you do it?

NIKOLAI: That's a stupid question.

TANYA: Just—

NIKOLAI: He would never ask—

TANYA: Just answer me, Nikolai.

NIKOLAI: Yes.

TANYA: You would.

NIKOLAI: Yes.

TANYA: But I thought you were a temple of God.

NIKOLAI: What?

TANYA: So you would harm it? You would harm God's temple?

NIKOLAI: That's not—

TANYA: Yes, it is. That is what you're saying. Look, I'm not interested in fancy words, or, or foolish deeds, they get in the way. They mask you. When you talk like that I can't see you anymore, and that's all I want, Nikolai. I just want to see you. To see who you are.

NIKOLAI, *surprised, looks at her for a moment.*

NIKOLAI: I...

He pauses.

>   I don't think they're fancy. They're words. They have meaning. And when I hear them, and speak them, I feel as if a fire has been lit, inside me. I feel...strong. Alive. And I think...I think that feeling is God.

TANYA: God.

NIKOLAI: It *has* to be. And I don't care what happens next. I just want that feeling.

TANYA: And what if it isn't God? What if God is something else.

NIKOLAI: Like what.

TANYA: I don't know, like...

She pauses.

>   My father always says that God used to live in our house. "When your mother was alive," he says, "I used to see God every day. And He used to see me. And let me tell you—it wasn't always so good."

They smile. Suddenly, TANYA *reaches out and takes his hand. For a moment, she holds it. Then, a door bangs, off. They look up.*

That's my brother. Come on.

She gets up, moves to the door. He stays sitting. She turns back to him.

Nikolai?

Slight pause. Then he gets up, follows her out.

Scene Seven

A field. Night. SAVELY *waiting.* NIKOLAI *enters, on his way home. He doesn't see his father.*

SAVELY: Nikolai.

NIKOLAI *stops.*

NIKOLAI: What do you want.

SAVELY: I want to talk to you. Just for a moment.

NIKOLAI: I have to get home.

SAVELY: Home? What do you mean? What home?

NIKOLAI *begins to leave.*

Wait. Nikolai, please.

Slight pause. NIKOLAI *doesn't leave.*

What were you doing in there?

NIKOLAI: None of your business.

SAVELY: Who were you talking to?

NIKOLAI *just looks at him.*

> Are you all right?

NIKOLAI: I'm fine.

SAVELY: What were you doing? What are you up to?

NIKOLAI: Nothing.

SAVELY: You're lying.

NIKOLAI: Father—

SAVELY: Tell me what you're up to!

NIKOLAI *turns, begins to leave.*

> *(Furious.)* Don't turn your back to me!

NIKOLAI *stops.*

> Don't you dare!

NIKOLAI *turns, looks at his father.*

> I've been following you. Did you know that? All night I've been watching you go into houses. House after house. *(Slight pause.)* Tell me what's happening.

NIKOLAI: I can't.

SAVELY: What are you doing in all of these houses? What are you saying?

NIKOLAI: Father—

SAVELY: Tell me.

NIKOLAI: I can't.

SAVELY: What are they making you say?

NIKOLAI: *(Not looking at him.)* I'm not supposed to talk to you.

SAVELY: Says who.

NIKOLAI: You can't be trusted.

SAVELY: What? Says who? Who said that? Nikolai?

NIKOLAI *says nothing.*

> I don't understand. I don't understand what's happening.

Pause.

> I'm sorry Nikolai. Whatever I did, and said, I'm sorry. I want you to come home now. I don't want you out here at night, talking to people, going in houses. You should be home.

NIKOLAI: *(Quiet.)* You didn't do anything.

SAVELY: What?

NIKOLAI: It has nothing to do with you. I don't care if you drink. Or smoke. Or sin.

SAVELY: You don't.

NIKOLAI *shakes his head.*

> Then why are we standing here? Eh? In a field. The middle of the night. Come on, let's go home.

NIKOLAI *doesn't move.*

> Nikolai, please. I'm saying: I don't know what to do. I need your help.

He drops to his knees.

ACT ONE—31

NIKOLAI: What are you doing.

SAVELY: I'm begging you.

NIKOLAI: *Don't.*

SAVELY: Stop what you're doing. Come home.

NIKOLAI: Get up.

SAVELY: It's not important! I know you think that it is, but it isn't.

NIKOLAI: Stop it.

SAVELY: Listen to me! They're just words, ideas, they're...look. *(He picks up some soil.)* Look at this. Eh? This is important. Remember? The *soil.*

NIKOLAI: I have to go.

NIKOLAI *exits.*

SAVELY: *(After him.)* Wait! Nikolai wait!

SAVELY *stays on his knees.*

Nikolai! *(Holding out hands.)* Look....My hands....

SAVELY, *still on his knees, looks after* NIKOLAI *for several long moments. Then, finally, he gets painfully to his feet, and limps off in the opposite direction.*

Scene Eight

NAKASHIDZE's *office*. NAKASHIDZE *enters, trailed by* GUBANOFF *and* ZUBKOFF. NAKASHIDZE *is in an excellent mood.*

GUBANOFF: We just need a moment.

ZUBKOFF: It's urgent, Governor.

GUBANOFF: Very urgent.

ZUBKOFF: It's an emergency.

GUBANOFF: Possibly a crisis.

ZUBKOFF: We thought you should know right away—

NAKASHIDZE: *(Interrupting.)* Do you know a man named Lebedev? He's a soldier.

GUBANOFF: Ah.

ZUBKOFF: Yes.

NAKASHIDZE: Do you know what he's done?

GUBANOFF: He's not one of ours.

NAKASHIDZE: I'm sorry?

ZUBKOFF: That's right—

NAKASHIDZE: Not one of yours?

ZUBKOFF: He's a fanatic.

NAKASHIDZE: A what?

GUBANOFF: A fanatic. Governor—

NAKASHIDZE: I don't understand. He's refusing to fight. He's refusing to serve the Tsar. He's professing his love of God and peace. And you call him a fanatic? I would have called him a Doukhobor.

ZUBKOFF: Governor, please—

NAKASHIDZE: You surprise me, gentlemen. I expected you to admire this man. I didn't expect you to call him names.

NAKASHIDZE *smiles at them. He is enjoying himself.*

ZUBKOFF: *(Slight pause. Patient.)* The reason he put down his gun is because he is loyal to Verigin.

NAKASHIDZE: Verigin?

ZUBKOFF: Yes.

NAKASHIDZE: *Peter* Verigin?

ZUBKOFF: Yes.

NAKASHIDZE: Didn't we exile him?

ZUBKOFF: Governor—

NAKASHIDZE: Yes, I'm sure we did. To Siberia.

ZUBKOFF: *(Losing his patience.)* He has established a network. Of couriers, who travel to him, in his exile, and bring back his words. He has managed, despite his absence, and against our expectations, to build up a following, a large following, of fanatic supporters who are willing to do almost anything in his name. You see, Governor, he has become a martyr. And as a result, he is more dangerous now than ever.

GUBANOFF: That's right. A martyr.

ZUBKOFF: We believe that his people are mobilizing.

GUBANOFF: A military force.

ZUBKOFF: They want our money.

GUBANOFF: They want the Orphan's Home.

ZUBKOFF: And they outnumber us. If they should attack, we would not be able to stop them. This is why we are here today.

GUBANOFF: We require your assistance, Governor.

ZUBKOFF: It is an emergency.

Pause. NAKASHIDZE *looks at them.*

NAKASHIDZE: Doukhobors.

ZUBKOFF: Yes.

NAKASHIDZE: Mobilizing.

ZUBKOFF: Yes.

NAKASHIDZE: I don't believe it.

ZUBKOFF: We have proof.

ZUBKOFF *gestures to* GUBANOFF, *who exits.*

NAKASHIDZE: What kind of proof.

ZUBKOFF: We've heard reports.

NAKASHIDZE: Reports?

ZUBKOFF: With your permission, Governor.

GUBANOFF *has returned, with* SAVELY.

GUBANOFF: This man's name is Kalmakoff.

ZUBKOFF: His wife and son are fanatics.

ACT ONE—35

GUBANOFF: *(To* SAVELY.*)* Tell the Governor what you told us.

SAVELY *hesitates.*

Quickly.

SAVELY: Vasily Verigin came to my house.

GUBANOFF: *(To* NAKASHIDZE.*)* Brother of Peter.

SAVELY: He spoke....

SAVELY *hesitates.*

NAKASHIDZE: Yes?

SAVELY: Please. I must have your promise. That my family will not be harmed.

ZUBKOFF: Savely—

NAKASHIDZE: *(To* ZUBKOFF.*)* That's all right.

SAVELY: I don't want to put them at risk.

NAKASHIDZE: Of course you don't. I promise.

SAVELY: *(Slight pause.)* He spoke to my wife and son. They thought I was out, but I came back. I didn't hear everything.

NAKASHIDZE: What did you hear.

SAVELY: Something about weapons. Guns. Preparations. They refuse to tell me.

NAKASHIDZE: Did you ask them?

SAVELY: Yes sir.

NAKASHIDZE: And they don't obey you?

SAVELY: *(Slight pause.)* No sir.

NAKASHIDZE: Did they mention a date?

SAVELY: Yes sir. June 29th. St. Peter's Day.

Pause. NAKASHIDZE *studies* SAVELY *for a moment, thinking.*

ZUBKOFF: You see, Governor? This is why we need help.

GUBANOFF: Immediately.

ZUBKOFF: We want you to send us some soldiers.

GUBANOFF: *(Glancing at* ZUBKOFF.*)* Well, not necessarily soldiers. A dozen policemen—

ZUBKOFF: More than a dozen.

GUBANOFF: *(To* ZUBKOFF.*)* But, Alyosha—

ZUBKOFF: I'd say at least several hundred. On horseback.

GUBANOFF: Horseback?

NAKASHIDZE *has begun writing something. He speaks without looking up.*

NAKASHIDZE: Thank you, gentlemen, that will be all. Good day.

ZUBKOFF: You won't regret this, Governor. I promise.

GUBANOFF: Governor, I—

ZUBKOFF: Thank you. Good day.

They begin to leave.

NAKASHIDZE: Leave the peasant.

ZUBKOFF: *(Stopping.)* I'm sorry?

NAKASHIDZE: *(Writing, not looking up.)* The peasant. Leave him with me.

GUBANOFF: But he's only—

ZUBKOFF: Of course. Certainly. Thank you, Governor.

ZUBKOFF *pulls* GUBANOFF *off.* SAVELY *remains standing, clearly frightened.* NAKASHIDZE *continues writing, doesn't acknowledge him for several long moments. Finally, he looks up, looks at* SAVELY. *Pause.*

NAKASHIDZE: Are you a farmer?

SAVELY: Sir?

NAKASHIDZE: A farmer. Are you a farmer.

SAVELY: *(Slight pause.)* Yes sir.

NAKASHIDZE: Yes. Good. You work hard.

SAVELY: Yes sir.

NAKASHIDZE: Yes, I'm sure you do. And you believe in God, don't you.

SAVELY: Yes sir.

NAKASHIDZE: God, living peacefully, working hard. Yes?

SAVELY: Sir.

NAKASHIDZE: You don't like politics. You just want to mind your own business. You want to love your family. Grow your...crops.

He pauses.

What was your name again?

SAVELY: Kalmakoff, sir. Savely.

NAKASHIDZE: *(Making a note.)* Kalmakoff. And you have a son.

SAVELY: Yes sir.

NAKASHIDZE: And his name is Kalmakoff too.

SAVELY *says nothing.*

Mm?

SAVELY: Yes sir.

NAKASHIDZE: First name?

SAVELY: *(Pauses.)* Nikolai.

NAKASHIDZE: Nikolai Kalmakoff.

SAVELY: Yes sir.

NAKASHIDZE: Thank you. *(Slight pause.)* May I tell you something? I admire you. I have a profound respect for you, Mr. Kalmakoff. I believe that you are a good man. Truly good. A model Russian. If only there were more of you in this world. Mm? More of you, and less of me.

SAVELY *says nothing. He stands before* **NAKASHIDZE**, *confused and frightened.*

Do I surprise you? What if I said that I wanted to be you. That I wanted your goodness. Your belief. Would you be shocked? What if I told you that I don't want to be corrupt. Immoral. Concerned with personal gain. I don't want to be expedient. I don't want to be ruthless. I don't want to be violent.

Let me give you an example. When you said before that I must promise. Remember? Promise not to harm your son, your Nikolai. And I said "yes, I promise, he will come to no harm." That is a perfect example. I want to be the kind of man who, in that situation, does not lie. You see? Who says

"No, I'm sorry, I cannot promise that. If you give me his name, then he will come to harm." You see Mr. Kalmakoff? That's what you would have said. Mm? If you were me? You would have told the truth.

Because, I mean, be honest: can you trust me now? Can you respect me?

SAVELY *just looks at him.*

Can you?

SAVELY *says nothing. Pause.*

All right. Thank you, Mr. Kalmakoff. Good day.

SAVELY: Please sir—

NAKASHIDZE: Yes?

SAVELY: I....

NAKASHIDZE: Yes?

Pause.

SAVELY: Good day sir.

NAKASHIDZE: Good day.

SAVELY *exits.* NAKASHIDZE *watches him go.*

Scene Nine

A sudden explosion. Leaping flames, the sound of a loud, roaring bonfire.

A Doukhobor choir sings; thousands of voices.

NIKOLAI *stands on the stage, singing passionately, the flames dancing on his face, his eyes wild. He has several weapons. One by one, he throws them on the fire.*

The sound of galloping hooves, shouts, cries, the crack of whips, gunfire. The singing rises to a crescendo.

Then blackout. All sounds cease instantly, except for NIKOLAI, *who keeps singing.*

Scene Ten

Early morning. NIKOLAI *stands next to the dead fire. He has been badly beaten. He continues singing in a hoarse voice.* NAKASHIDZE *stands near him. He has a riding whip. He watches* NIKOLAI *for several moments.*

NAKASHIDZE: Your name?

NIKOLAI *doesn't answer, keeps singing.*

Your name?

NIKOLAI *keeps singing.*

Be quiet.

NIKOLAI *continues singing.*

Your name is Kalmakoff. Nikolai Savelyevitch Kalmakoff. I'm acquainted with your father.

NIKOLAI *stops singing, looks at* NAKASHIDZE.

Does that interest you? Do I have your attention?

Let's be absolutely clear. All right? You are a peasant. I am the Tsar's governor. I could have you hurt or maimed or killed without consequence or qualm. Is that clear?

NIKOLAI: *(Quiet.)* You will be in Hell.

NAKASHIDZE: I'm sorry?

NIKOLAI: You will be in Hell. I will be in Paradise. That is the difference between us.

NAKASHIDZE: *(Delighted.)* Really. Oh I see. So, let me get this clear. You are chosen, I am doomed. You are blessed, I am cursed. That's what you believe?

NIKOLAI: "If they persecute me they will persecute you."

NAKASHIDZE: Pardon?

NIKOLAI: "Do not be afraid of them that kill the body, as the soul cannot be killed. The Christian argues with no one, assaults no one. The Christian suffers silently without contradiction or violence and thus overcomes evil."

Pause. NAKASHIDZE *looks at him.*

NAKASHIDZE: You're very sure of yourself, aren't you Nikolai. Very certain. It's in your eyes. The absolute...conviction. It must be wonderful to be so sure. To see the world so...simply. Christian and evil.

To be honest, they frighten me, your eyes. Just a little. They say: "I am capable of anything."

Are you Nikolai? Mm? Of anything?

No response.

Let's examine this further. Christian and evil: which one are you. Well, it's obvious, the Christian. After all, you burned your arms. Last night, you gathered up your weapons and your guns, and you burned them. In bonfires. You burned them. You showed the world, the entire world, just how good and peaceful and Christian you are. Which leaves me to be the evil. It makes sense. I responded with violence. Didn't I. My soldiers are killing your people. Even as we speak. They are looting your villages. They are raping your women.

How am I doing. Do you agree? *(Points to* NIKOLAI.*)* Christian. *(Points to himself.)* Evil.

Except for one thing. You knew. You knew what would happen. You knew that if I was presented with rebellion, I would respond with force. It was a given. And yet, you went ahead. Ah hah. So, the question now becomes: is this pacifism? Or is it suicide? Is the violence mine, or yours? Perhaps we had it wrong. Perhaps you're not the Christian after all. Perhaps you're the evil. Perhaps, in fact, I'm the Christian. *I'm* the pacifist. Perhaps I understand that in this world peace is won not by submitting to violence but by defeating it. Not through weakness, but strength. Perhaps I see the need for soldiers: to eliminate killing. Perhaps—

NIKOLAI *starts singing again, drowning him out.* NAKASHIDZE *watches for a moment. Then, he speaks over top of the singing.*

Do you think I am incapable Nikolai? Of having beliefs? Is that what you think?

NIKOLAI *keeps singing.*

Be quiet.

NIKOLAI *keeps singing.*

Be quiet!

NIKOLAI *continues to sing. Suddenly,* NAKASHIDZE *attacks* NIKOLAI. *He hits him in the stomach.* NIKOLAI *falls.* NAKASHIDZE *kicks him.*

NIKOLAI *lies on the ground.*

> I know what you're doing. You want to be the victim, don't you. Because victims are never at fault. They are holy. They are Christian. And, in order to be a victim, you must have an oppressor, yes? Someone to blame. And you've chosen me. I'm to play Pilate to your Christ.
>
> Well, I refuse. Anyone can suffer, Nikolai. The difficult thing is to generate peace. It takes effort, skill, courage. Faith. You can't just lie there, you have to get up. On your feet. I'm going to give you that chance. Right now. This is what you have to do. Stand up. Right now. Stand up and swear an oath. An oath of allegiance, hand on heart. If you can do that, I will call off my soldiers. Can you do that? Hm? Do you have the strength? The courage?

NIKOLAI *lies on the floor, not moving.*

> Stand up, Nikolai.

NIKOLAI *doesn't move.*

> Stand up.
>
> Stand up.

NIKOLAI *stirs. Slowly and painfully, he gets to his feet. He coughs.* NAKASHIDZE *watches. He waits until* NIKOLAI *is standing more or less upright.*

> Well done. Feels good, doesn't it. Now, repeat after me. I, Nikolai Kalmakoff.

NIKOLAI *is silent.*

> I, Nikolai Kalmakoff.

NIKOLAI *coughs.*

> I can't hear you, Nikolai. You must speak clearly.

NIKOLAI: I....

NAKASHIDZE: I what.

NIKOLAI: I, Nikolai....

NAKASHIDZE: Nikolai what.

NIKOLAI: I, Nikolai Kalmakoff.

NAKASHIDZE: Do pledge allegiance.

NIKOLAI: Do pledge allegiance.

NAKASHIDZE: To the Tsar of Russia.

NIKOLAI: To....

NAKASHIDZE: To the Tsar of Russia.

NIKOLAI: To....

NAKASHIDZE: The Tsar—

NIKOLAI: To God. To God our heavenly father and to Jesus Christ and Verigin. To Peter Verigin: the Living Christ.

NIKOLAI *coughs violently. He falls to his knees, coughing, doubled over, in terrible pain.* NAKASHIDZE *just watches. Finally* NIKOLAI *stops. He lies on the ground, breathing painfully.*

NAKASHIDZE: *(Pause.)* Is this what you call peace?

NIKOLAI *looks up at* NAKASHIDZE. *For a moment, they look at each other. Then blackout.*

Scene Eleven

The office of Sir Clifford Sifton, Ottawa. SIFTON *and* MAVOR.

SIFTON: Professor Mavor, do come in.

MAVOR: Minister.

SIFTON: Hello. Lovely to see you again. How was your train.

MAVOR: We sat in Kingston for over an hour.

SIFTON: Good heavens!

MAVOR: But, I managed to catch up on my correspondence.

SIFTON: Ha ha! Well done! Please. Sit down.

MAVOR *sits.*

Now. What would you like. Whiskey? I have scotch.

MAVOR: No thank you.

SIFTON: Sure?

MAVOR: Yes.

SIFTON: Tea?

MAVOR: Thank you.

SIFTON: Excellent.

SIFTON *pours tea for both of them. He has an elaborate tea ritual.*

MAVOR: As a matter of fact, I was writing a letter to Tolstoy. In Russia.

SIFTON: Really, Tolstoy!

MAVOR: I've known him for several years. An intensely political man.

SIFTON: Indeed.

MAVOR: Not to mention a brilliant author. One of the greatest thinkers, not to mention *Christians* this century has produced.

SIFTON: Mm.

MAVOR: You would agree then, Minister?

SIFTON: Eh?

MAVOR: That he's a great man?

SIFTON: Tolstoy? No question. One lump or two?

MAVOR: Just one.

SIFTON: *(Adding sugar, stirring.)* Just...one. There you are.

MAVOR: Thank you.

They take a moment and sip their tea. SIFTON *enjoys his tea immensely.*

Now, Minister. The reason I'm here. I assume—

MAVOR *breaks off as* SIFTON *takes another sip. He waits until the cup is back on the saucer.*

I assume you received my package.

SIFTON: Yes. The Doukhobors.

MAVOR: This is why I've been corresponding with Tolstoy. You see, he's taken rather a shine to them.

SIFTON: Has he.

MAVOR: He calls them "The True Christians."

SIFTON: Does he.

MAVOR: He's been writing letters to *The Times*. Raising money. Telling how the Doukhobors have been kicked off their land. Exiled.

SIFTON: Yes, you mentioned.

MAVOR: How they're dying by the hundreds. Most of malaria, many of starvation, malnutrition. How the Tsar, it seems, intends to exterminate them. Like rats.

Slight pause.

Now, I think you know what I am about to suggest.

SIFTON: I do indeed.

MAVOR: They are excellent farmers. Possibly the best in Russia. And you need farmers.

SIFTON: Yes.

MAVOR: They require land, obviously. But they require more than land. They have been rendered destitute. They are helpless. They are in need of help. Tolstoy has been helping. But Tolstoy is not enough. He needs allies. Men who share his vision. His Christianity. His...greatness.

SIFTON: Ah.

He pauses.

Yes, I've gone through your package, Professor. I found it...fascinating. What a story! And it's clear, no question, they would be an asset. Yes, I'm a great fan of East Europeans.

Slight pause.

I do, however, have some...questions...*(Flipping pages.)* Just little things...one or two words that....Ah. Yes. Here. "Pacifist."

MAVOR: That's right.

SIFTON: And over here. "Communal."

MAVOR: Yes, that's right, they are communal. You would have to waive the Homestead Act.

SIFTON: I see.

MAVOR: And exempt them from military service.

SIFTON: I see.

MAVOR: I believe there is a precedent—

SIFTON: Yes, the Mennonites.

MAVOR: Minister, you would be saving hundreds of lives.

SIFTON: Would I.

MAVOR: Possibly thousands.

SIFTON: Well, that does sound attractive.

He pauses.

You do understand, Professor, I want nothing but the best.

MAVOR: Of course.

SIFTON: It is a great responsibility. A new society! How wonderful! And it is vital that we set the right note, the proper tone. It must be a moral society. It must be an industrious society. Open-minded, tolerant, inclusive, a foundation. The decisions we make today will *resonate,* for hundreds of years. Generations to come will look back on us and say: Yes.

Good job. Well done. Are you with me, Professor?

MAVOR: Yes.

SIFTON: May I ask you to be frank?

MAVOR: Of course.

SIFTON: These Doukhobors. They will...behave themselves.

MAVOR: Minister, we're talking about a society literally without sin.

SIFTON: Are we.

MAVOR: A society that's managed to escape the modern world, that lives with a kind of Biblical purity, a moral directness, a simplicity. Each man loving his brother as himself. I must say I find it inspiring. Who would have thought that halfway 'round the world, in a distant mountain range in Russia, there existed Utopia.

SIFTON: Utopia.

MAVOR: Yes. A Utopia which they carry with them, wherever they live.

SIFTON: And you think they could carry it here, to Canada. This Utopia.

MAVOR: Yes. I do.

SIFTON: *(Slight pause.)* Well then, we'd better have them.

MAVOR: Excellent.

SIFTON: Utopia is something I'd like to see.

Scene Twelve

NIKOLAI and ANNA, in exile. It is very hot. ANNA is lying down: she has malaria. NIKOLAI kneels, next to her. He is in rough shape: feverish, with a strange intensity.

NIKOLAI: For the sake of Thee, Oh Lord,
    I loved the narrow gate;
    I left the material life;
    I left father and mother;
    I left brother and sister;
    I left my whole race and tribe;

    For the sake of Thee, Oh Lord,
    I bear hardness and persecution;
    I bear scorn and slander;
    I am hungry and thirsty;
    I am walking naked—

He breaks off, coughing. TANYA has entered, and has listened to some of the psalm.

TANYA: Nikolai?

NIKOLAI: *(Turns.)* Tanya.

TANYA: Are you all right?

NIKOLAI stands. They look at each other. They both seem dazed, disoriented.

    Hello.

NIKOLAI: Hello.

TANYA: Are you all right?

NIKOLAI: Yes. Are you?

TANYA: You look terrible. *(Looks at ANNA.)* Is that your mother?

NIKOLAI: Yes.

TANYA: How is she?

NIKOLAI: She has the fever.

TANYA: *(Moving to her.)* Is she dying?

NIKOLAI: I don't know.

TANYA: Have you been bathing her?

NIKOLAI: Uh huh.

TANYA: Her forehead?

NIKOLAI: Yes.

TANYA: You have to keep her cool.

NIKOLAI: I know.

TANYA: My father died on the road. I told him he was carrying too much. He wouldn't listen, he wouldn't leave anything behind, he...

Pause.

It's filthy in here.

NIKOLAI: I know.

TANYA: It stinks. It's foul.

Pause. NIKOLAI *just looks at her. He sways slightly.*

Did you know this would happen?

NIKOLAI: Yes.

TANYA: Then why did you do it? What did you achieve? Why have you brought us here? Why are we hungry? Why are we sick? Where are our homes? Where are our families? Why are we dying? What do you *want?*

NIKOLAI: A narrow path.

TANYA: A what?

NIKOLAI: A narrow path. We achieved a narrow path, voluntary sorrow, a life of a pilgrim, a life...*(He is about to collapse.)* A life...of poverty....

NIKOLAI *topples. He falls to the floor, lies there in a heap. He coughs.* **TANYA** *moves to him. She cradles his head in her lap. She bathes his forehead.*

TANYA: I wept this morning. For the first time. Guess why. Because I sold the candlesticks. I traded them, for breakfast. I was hungry. They'd been in my family for hundreds of years, passed down. It was always my job to polish them, to keep them nice. When my father died, I didn't weep. But this morning I wept. For those candlesticks.

Pause.

Look. I know what you're going to say. We have to suffer. All of us, to overcome sin, and find salvation. But the truth is, Nikolai, I don't know what that means. What does that mean? And this salvation: when do we get it? Is this it? This right now? Because, you know...this isn't so good.

NIKOLAI: Have you ever heard of Canada?

TANYA: No.

NIKOLAI: It's a country. Across the sea somewhere. It's in America.

TANYA: What about it.

NIKOLAI: We're going there.

TANYA: Who is.

ACT ONE—53

NIKOLAI: Everyone. The people. We're leaving Russia. We're going to Canada. In ships. It's true. They just decided.

TANYA *looks at him, trying to judge if he's delirious.*

TANYA: I don't believe you.

NIKOLAI: Look.

He pulls a piece of paper from his pocket, shows it to her.

See this word? Canada. Here it is again. And over here. And over here. *(Pointing.)* Canada. Canada. Canada. They're giving us land. Enough for everyone. Enough to build our villages. And farm.

TANYA: Why would they give us land?

NIKOLAI: Because. We suffered.

TANYA *takes the piece of paper and, unable to read, stares at it.* ANNA *speaks, in a clear voice, from her delirium.*

ANNA: A time of grief...a time of grief shall come...grief and trials, before the glory...a time of grief...before the glory...a time of grief....

Pause.

TANYA: I have a question. This Canada. There's land there?

NIKOLAI: Yes.

TANYA: Is there sun?

NIKOLAI: What?

TANYA: Sun. Is there sun there. In Canada.

NIKOLAI: Yes.

TANYA: Is there rain?

Slight pause.

NIKOLAI: *(Smiles.)* I think so, yes.

TANYA: That's good. Sun *and* rain.

NIKOLAI: There's no soldiers there. No soldiers, and no government. There's just sun, and rain, and soil, and....

TANYA: What.

NIKOLAI: And freedom.

TANYA: Freedom.

NIKOLAI: And houses.

TANYA: And—

NIKOLAI: And fields. And clouds. And....

Pause. They look at each other.

TANYA: I'm going to need a husband.

NIKOLAI: What?

TANYA: In Canada. I'll need a husband. Someone to live with. Someone to have children with.

NIKOLAI: You will?

TANYA: Yes.

NIKOLAI: Oh.

TANYA: From now on, we're together. All right? We're not alone.

NIKOLAI reaches out to her.

END OF ACT ONE.

ACT ONE—55

Leo Tolstoy (1828-1910) reading letters from his Doukhobor friends in Canada.

Lunch time: borstch and souhari (dried bread) on board the freighter "Lake Huron" to Canada, January, 1899.

First shipload of Doukhobors to land in Canada on January 21, 1899 (detail).

ACT TWO

With sickles they reaped their first Canadian harvest in 1899. The men were away building the railroad—earning money to buy essentials to survive the coming winter.

Act Two—Scene One

Thin singing in the dark. Lights up on open prairie. Wind and snow. ZIBAROFF, *barefoot, is preaching to a large group of Doukhobors. He is in a frenzy.*

ZIBAROFF: We are pilgrims! We are prepared for miracles! Though we be blasted by the freezing wind, we are not cold! Though we have nothing to eat, we are not hungry! Though we find ourselves in strange and foreign lands...we are not afraid! God will feed us! God will keep us warm! We will meet Him in Paradise! The land of sun! And we shall harvest golden fruit from golden trees. And all the animals will speak to us. And—*(He has a vision.)* Ah! I see him! I see Jesus! Look, he is beckoning, to all of us. He wants us to follow! Jesus will lead us to Paradise!

Scene Two

SIFTON'S *office, Ottawa.* MAVOR *sits, waiting.* SIFTON *enters, with a newspaper. He is clearly upset. He moves directly to the teapot, pours himself a desperately needed cup of tea.*

SIFTON: Ah. Professor.

MAVOR: Good morning, Minister.

SIFTON: *(Brisk.)* What would you like. Tea? Coffee?

MAVOR: No. Thank you, I—

SIFTON: *(Interrupting.)* Have you seen the papers, Professor?

MAVOR: Yes.

SIFTON: Good. Because so has the Opposition. So has every single member of the House of Commons. I've had a most interesting morning.

MAVOR: Yes—

SIFTON: In Question Period, most interesting. Do you know what they asked me? Who on earth, they asked, are these Doukhobors? Why are several thousand Russian peasants marching across the open prairie, at the end of October, without adequate food, clothing, or shelter?

MAVOR: Minister—

SIFTON: Why, they asked, are government officers required, at great expense, to save them from death by starvation and exposure?

MAVOR: Please—

SIFTON: Tell us, they cried, why did you bring them here? What have you done?

MAVOR: And what was your reply.

SIFTON: Reply?

MAVOR: Yes.

SIFTON: I had no reply, Professor. None at all. It was more than embarrassing. It was humiliating.

MAVOR: I should have thought you'd defend them.

SIFTON: Defend them?

MAVOR: You might have replied that the Doukhobors are under terrific stress.

SIFTON: Stress?

MAVOR: You might have spoken about the poverty, the back breaking labour, the language barrier, the difficult winters.

SIFTON: Professor—

MAVOR: You might have said, yes, there's bound to be problems. They're an idealistic, uncompromising people. But they're also good. They're worth it. I should have thought you would show more determination. More character.

SIFTON *just looks at him.*

Look, Minister. We have to be patient.

SIFTON: I have been patient, Professor, I've been nothing *but*—

MAVOR: *(Interrupting.)* We have to consider the point that it might not be *them* that's the problem. It might be us. *(Slight pause.)* I propose we set up a meeting. With one of their people. Smooth out some of the...wrinkles. I can make all the arrangements.

SIFTON: Yes. fine. Just...please...find someone rational. All right?

Scene Three

A meeting hall. A table. On the table: bread, salt, water. Several Doukhobors, including NIKOLAI *and* ZIBAROFF *are behind the table.* NIKOLAI *has a newspaper. They address a large group of Doukhobors.*

NIKOLAI: *(To* ZIBAROFF.*)* Are you crazy? Do you realize what you have done? *(To the meeting.)* We are now a laughing-stock, in this country. A punch-line. Those crazy Doukhobors.

ZIBAROFF: We are—

NIKOLAI: *(Interrupting, holding up newspaper.)* The Manitoba Free Press: "...hundreds of men, with the light of insanity in their eyes, roaming whither and for what they know not, driven by a belief that brings the dark ages into the twentieth century!"

ZIBAROFF: That is—

NIKOLAI: *(Not stopping.)* Why do you think the government wants a meeting? They think they've made a mistake! And frankly, I don't blame them!

ZIBAROFF: I wish to speak.

NIKOLAI: If I were them—

ZIBAROFF: *(Over-riding him.)* I wish to speak. You have spoken.

NIKOLAI *looks at him for a moment. Then he sits.* ZIBAROFF *turns to the meeting. He has a telegram.*

> Friends. Brothers. This is the telegram. Here it is. From the Government of Canada, written in English. It says: come to Ottawa, come to our meeting...or else.

NIKOLAI: *(Standing.)* That's not what it says.

ZIBAROFF: I am speaking.

NIKOLAI: But it doesn't say that. It's very polite.

ZIBAROFF *looks at him.*

> All right. *(He sits.)*

ZIBAROFF: They ask us for a response. Well, my friends, I have a response. *This* is my response.

He tears the telegram in half. NIKOLAI *almost gets up again, but restrains himself.*

> We must not forget! Yes we are in a new country. It isn't Russia, there isn't a Tsar, but there is a government, my friends, and we do not trust governments!

NIKOLAI: *(Back on his feet.)* Wait a second—

ZIBAROFF: *(Over-riding him.)* How does it begin? With a telegram. A meeting. "Come to Ottawa." And so we go, and this, and that, and then it's "Oh, and by the way, we want you to swear this oath."

NIKOLAI: *(Shaking head.)* No.

ZIBAROFF: "Oh, and by the way, we want to *conscript* you."

NIKOLAI: That's—

ZIBAROFF: We cannot serve two masters! What would Peter Verigin say, if he saw this telegram? He would say: "Ignore it. Do not go." He would tell us: "We are subjects of God. We must serve God. We must cast away our riches, and our worldly goods. We must free our animals from servitude, and we must leave this place, this barren place, and search, however we can, for Paradise. The land of God. Where the sun is ever warm." That's what he would say! And I tell you, friends, I promise you, that Verigin will join us there! The Lordly! He will live with us, in Paradise! We must prepare the way!

ZIBAROFF *sits, abruptly. Scattered clapping.* NIKOLAI, *who has watched* ZIBAROFF'*s performance in silence, now stands. He waits for silence.*

NIKOLAI: *(Pause.)* Well. I don't agree. I don't think Verigin would say that. Any of that. And you know, I don't think he'd be very...proud. Of us. Of how we're getting on.

He pauses.

I wonder what he would say. If he were here, in this room. If it were *he* that stood in front of you today, instead of me. Perhaps he would turn to Zibaroff here. "Tell me, Ivan," he'd say, "How would you *define* this paradise? A place where there is land? A place where we can cultivate? And build, and grow? A place where we can live in honest toil? Is it a place where we no longer have to suffer?"

Slight pause.

And then perhaps he'd turn. And point outside. And say to Ivan: "Look. Look out there. Stretching out in all directions. Under the snow. Beneath the wind. Surrounding us. You don't have to search any further, my friend. You've found it. You've discovered Paradise. It's name…is Canada."

He looks out at the meeting.

I believe it's a gift. All this. Not from Ottawa. From God. Because we suffered. Perhaps we should act a little more grateful.

He looks at ZIBAROFF. *He picks up the torn bits of telegram.*

I propose that we accept this invitation. That we go to Ottawa, and tell them we are *happy*.

We must stop this madness. We must work together. So that when, at last, he arrives, Peter Verigin will be *proud*. Of us. His people.

ZIBAROFF *rises, to speak. But someone has started singing a psalm. Voices join in.*

ZIBAROFF: My friends—

The singing gets louder. ZIBAROFF *looks at* NIKOLAI, *who starts singing along. Finally,* ZIBAROFF *is forced to sing too. The meeting ends: the people parade out, singing.* NIKOLAI *remains behind, looking after them.* ANNA *approaches.* TANYA *is in the background.*

ANNA: You're a good speaker.

NIKOLAI: *(Sees her.)* Mother.

ANNA: You make a good impression.

NIKOLAI: Really?

ANNA: Everyone is impressed. They talk about you. They agree with what you say.

NIKOLAI: *(Looking after* ZIBAROFF.*)* I hope so.

ANNA: Nikolai.

He looks at her.

    I'm proud of you.

He smiles.

    Come here.

NIKOLAI *goes to her.*

    You don't believe me?

NIKOLAI: Sure.

ANNA: I'm your mother.

NIKOLAI: I know.

ANNA: You're becoming an important man. It's true. Don't argue. Why don't *you* go.

NIKOLAI: What?

ANNA: To Ottawa. This meeting. You should go.

NIKOLAI: *I* should?

ANNA: Yes. Because you're linked. You and Peter Verigin, you always have been. Why? Because you have his *faith*. And then you can go to Siberia.

NIKOLAI: Mother—

ANNA: Why not? Stop in Ottawa, have your meeting, and then...keep going. All the way to Siberia. Sure you could. They have to send someone.

TANYA: *(Approaching.)* What's this?

ANNA: *(To* NIKOLAI.*)* Because you're linked.

NIKOLAI: *(To* TANYA.*)* It's nothing.

ANNA: *(To* TANYA, *defiant.)* I was saying Nikolai should go to Siberia.

Slight pause. TANYA *with a hint of a smile.*

TANYA: Siberia.

ANNA: That's right. To bring us back the Living Christ. What's funny?

TANYA: Nothing.

ANNA: *(Getting angry.)* Someone has to go!

TANYA: I know—

ANNA: He can't just *leave.*

TANYA: You're right—

ANNA: He can't just walk across the ocean. Someone has to get him!

TANYA: Yes—

ANNA: It might as well be Nikolai.

TANYA: That's right. It might as well. You're absolutely right.

ANNA *is unsure if* TANYA *is making fun of her.*

ANNA: I have work to do. *(To* NIKOLAI, *as she goes.)* Think about it.

ANNA *leaves.*

TANYA: *(Smiling.)* I'm sorry. I can't help it!

NIKOLAI: Neither can she.

TANYA: I know. I'm sorry.

NIKOLAI: So?

TANYA: So what.

NIKOLAI: So what did you think?

TANYA: About what? *(Slight pause.)* You know what I think.

NIKOLAI: Tanya—

TANYA: You know how to talk, you've always known how to talk. *(Slight pause.)* It makes me nervous.

NIKOLAI: What does.

TANYA: All of it. Zibaroff. *Verigin.* I mean, what is he going to do? When he gets here? Wave his hand, and everything will be perfect?

NIKOLAI: No—

TANYA: You're placing all your bets on him, that makes me nervous.

NIKOLAI: Tanya, we're like children. Look at us. We don't know *how* to act, we, we've been dropped here, in this country, where we can do anything, *anything!* Of *course* we're going to disagree! That's the point! What we need is leadership! That's all we—

He realizes, stops.

Am I talking again?

TANYA: Nikolai. You're not a child. You're a man. *(Slight pause.)*

Come here.

He goes to her.

I love you.

NIKOLAI: I love you.

TANYA: I don't want you to go to Siberia.

NIKOLAI: Okay.

TANYA: I don't want you going anywhere.

NIKOLAI: Okay.

TANYA: I want you staying here. Right...here.

Scene Four

SIFTON's *office, in Ottawa.* SIFTON, MAVOR, *and* NIKOLAI.

MAVOR: Minister, may I introduce Mr. Kalmakoff. Nikolai Savelyevitch. Nikolai, The Right Honourable Sir Clifford Sifton, Minister of the Interior.

SIFTON *speaks as if to a child.* NIKOLAI *speaks slowly, haltingly, with a thick Russian accent.*

SIFTON: Hello! Welcome to Ottawa.

NIKOLAI: *(Bows low.)* God be praised.

SIFTON: *(Not sure whether to bow in return.)* Yes. Thank you. Same to you.

MAVOR: Nikolai's English is surprisingly good.

NIKOLAI: I don't have many chance to speak with English.

SIFTON: Well you're doing brilliantly.

NIKOLAI: Thank you.

SIFTON: Smashing.

MAVOR: *(Slight pause.)* Well.

SIFTON: *(Gazing at* NIKOLAI.*)* I'm most interested in your people. I'm a great fan of East Europeans. Frankly, I don't know where this country would be without them, they've almost single-handedly opened up the west.

MAVOR: That's right.

SIFTON: Unfortunately they—you—also have your critics. People who believe that you aren't willing to integrate, to become...Canadian. They say, quite rightly, that we are building a new country, which, as such, requires unity.

MAVOR: Yes, but surely—

SIFTON: *(Not stopping.)* However. Their comments are all too often tinged with a racist overtone. Which I cannot abide. *(Slight pause.)* I'm not sure where I stand on integration. Somewhere in the middle, I suppose. As usual.

He smiles charmingly. There is a slight pause.

MAVOR: Mr. Kalmakoff has come with a request.

SIFTON: Has he.

MAVOR: It's regarding Peter Verigin.

SIFTON: Ah.

MAVOR: I spoke of the matter before, you may remember.

SIFTON: I do indeed.

MAVOR: Mr. Kalmakoff would like us to negotiate for his release. Personally, I think it's an excellent idea.

SIFTON: *(Suddenly.)* What can I give you?

MAVOR: I'm sorry?

SIFTON: Tea? *(To NIKOLAI.)* Yes? Tea?

NIKOLAI: Yes.

SIFTON: Professor?

MAVOR: Yes. Thank you.

NIKOLAI: Thank you.

SIFTON: *(Gestures for them to sit.)* Please.

They sit. SIFTON *serves the tea.*

MAVOR: As I was saying, Minister, bringing Peter Verigin to Canada, the re-uniting of the leader with the people, would have an unquestionably stabilizing effect.

SIFTON: *(Handing tea to MAVOR.)* Professor.

MAVOR: Thank you. Now, I've been in touch with Russia. I've made some enquiries. And I think it's possible.

SIFTON: *(To NIKOLAI.)* One lump or two?

NIKOLAI: Thank you.

MAVOR: All it seems to require is clout. Political clout.

SIFTON: *(Handing tea to NIKOLAI.)* There you are.

NIKOLAI: Thank you.

MAVOR: Such as you possess, Minister.

SIFTON: You flatter me, Professor.

MAVOR: Not at all. I'm simply stating the facts.

SIFTON *sips his tea.*

SIFTON: You know, it's rather embarrassing, but...I don't think there's anything that gives me greater satisfaction...than a good cup of tea.

Pause. *He has their full attention.*

(*To* NIKOLAI.) You've been in this country now for...five years?

NIKOLAI: Yes.

SIFTON: And you're doing rather well.

MAVOR: Extremely well.

SIFTON: You've built your villages, you've broken some land.

MAVOR: They built the railway.

SIFTON: I understand you're pacifists.

NIKOLAI: Yes.

SIFTON: Admirable. Very Christian. And...communists, too?

NIKOLAI: Yes.

MAVOR: Minister....

SIFTON: *(Ignoring him.)* Fascinating. Tell me, what does that mean, exactly?

MAVOR: I've explained it to you—

SIFTON: *(Interrupting, to* NIKOLAI.) Mr. Kalmakoff. Why don't you tell me what it means.

They both turn to him. Slight pause.

NIKOLAI: I wish to say. Doukhobors are happy in Canada. Happy. For Doukhobors, Canada is Paradise. Thank you.

Pause.

SIFTON: Yes. *(Pause.)* Look, Mr. Kalmakoff. I'd best be entirely frank. The west is filling up. Good, fertile land, such as yours, is becoming valuable. And a lot of people want it. *(To* MAVOR.*)* How much does he know about the Hamlet Clause?

MAVOR: Well, he—

SIFTON: *(Interrupting, to* NIKOLAI.*)* There is something called The Homestead Act. This is how it works. A man, a settler, registers for a piece of land. He is given three years to "improve" it. This means he must break it, till it, and live upon it. He must *homestead.* If he does so, he is allowed to own it. All right?

MAVOR: Minister—

SIFTON: Now. Your people were given special privileges. You are allowed to live and work, as you say, "together," communally, in villages, or "hamlets." As well, you are exempt from the responsibilities that come with owning land. Such as military service. That was the deal.

NIKOLAI: Yes.

SIFTON: However. Your land must still be registered. And it *must* be tilled. Up to this point, neither has occurred.

MAVOR: That's not true.

SIFTON: *Some* of it has been tilled, but some is not enough. Large tracts remain unbroken. And now there are people, voters, who are looking at this land, and *seeing* that it isn't tilled. And then they are looking at the book and seeing that it isn't *registered*. And when they are told about special privileges, they are getting upset. And complaining rather loudly.

MAVOR: They're not "privileges," Minister, they're *terms*. Of an agreement.

SIFTON: Which is in *peril*. Do you understand? Of being *revoked*.

Pause.

I support you, Mr. Kalmakoff. I can hold the wolves at bay. But you must do something for me. You must behave yourselves. All right? No more of these marches.

MAVOR: Minister—

SIFTON: And more importantly, you must sign. For your land. We must have your names in our book. Professor Mavor has agreed to travel out to get these names. You must help him. You must tell them to sign the book, and till the soil. Do you understand?

NIKOLAI: Yes.

SIFTON Can you do this?

NIKOLAI: Yes.

SIFTON: Good. Because otherwise—

NIKOLAI: I can do this.

SIFTON: Excellent. Because otherwise—

NIKOLAI: But I am only one.

SIFTON: I'm sorry?

NIKOLAI: I am only one. The people will not listen. Not to me.

SIFTON: They won't.

NIKOLAI: They will listen to Verigin. To Peter Verigin.

SIFTON: *(Pause.)* Ah.

NIKOLAI: Verigin will solve every problem.

SIFTON: Will he tell your people to sign?

NIKOLAI: He will solve every problem.

Pause.

MAVOR: By all reports, he's an excellent man.

SIFTON: Is he.

MAVOR: Tolstoy speaks most highly of him.

SIFTON: Does he.

MAVOR: Yes. Most highly.

Pause.

SIFTON: All right. Why not. One more can't hurt. Where is he, Siberia?

NIKOLAI: Yes.

SIFTON: Right! Siberia. No problem. We'll send for him.

NIKOLAI: Minister. I promise. Peter Verigin will take Doukhobors...and make them into Canadians.

Scene Five

A Doukhobor house: home of NIKOLAI *and* TANYA. *Table and chairs. On the table: bread, water, salt.* ANNA *can be heard, off, in the kitchen, singing.* TANYA *stands in the centre of the room, arms crossed, head down, listening to* ANNA. *She is furious. After several moments,* NIKOLAI *enters in a state of excitement.*

NIKOLAI: *(Entering.)* Tanya?

TANYA: She won't let me into the kitchen.

NIKOLAI: What?

TANYA: Who do you think? She won't let me into the kitchen!

NIKOLAI: Tanya.

TANYA: I've had enough of this. I'm serious—

NIKOLAI: What is she doing.

TANYA: She's cooking!

NIKOLAI: All right—

TANYA: What do you think she's doing! What is the matter with you!

NIKOLAI: Calm down.

TANYA: You calm down! I hate your mother Nikolai, all right? I hate her. God, the way she fawns on you—

NIKOLAI: Tanya—

TANYA: Someone should tell her: stop cooking! He's not going to eat it, he'll be full! "No he won't," she says, "He's been living in Siberia—"

NIKOLAI: He's coming here.

TANYA: I know he's coming, Nikolai, I know that!

NIKOLAI: No, I mean he's coming here.

TANYA: What?

NIKOLAI: *(Gesturing.)* Here.

TANYA: Here this village or here this house.

NIKOLAI: House.

TANYA: Here?

NIKOLAI: Here.

TANYA: When.

NIKOLAI: Now.

TANYA: Now?

NIKOLAI: Any second.

Slight pause. Frozen.

TANYA: Get the broom.

They spring into action. TANYA *opens a trunk, gets out linen and candlesticks, prepares the table.* NIKOLAI *sweeps. They talk as they work.*

TANYA: I thought he was coming on Sunday.

NIKOLAI: So did I. He sent a messenger to find me.

TANYA: Really? A messenger?

NIKOLAI: Uh huh.

TANYA: Why does he want to see you?

NIKOLAI: I don't know.

TANYA: Now don't get too excited.

NIKOLAI: Don't get excited! Peter Verigin is coming!

TANYA: I know—

NIKOLAI: He's coming to our house!

TANYA: Should I get changed?

NIKOLAI: No. Should I?

TANYA: No. You look good.

NIKOLAI: So do you.

A knock.

TANYA: That's him.

NIKOLAI: Okay.

TANYA: Now, just relax.

NIKOLAI: I am relaxed. You relax.

TANYA: Open the door.

NIKOLAI: I'm opening the door.

Slight pause. NIKOLAI *opens the door.* VERIGIN *stands in the doorway.*

VERIGIN: Good evening.

NIKOLAI: Good evening.

TANYA: *(Overlapping.)* Good evening.

VERIGIN: Do I have the right house? Kalmakoff?

NIKOLAI: Yes.

TANYA: That's us.

VERIGIN: Good. You received my message?

NIKOLAI: Yes, yes we did. Thank you.

TANYA: Please. Come in.

VERIGIN: Thank you.

Verigin enters.

NIKOLAI: I am Nikolai Savelyevitch, and this is my wife, Tanya Petrovna.

VERIGIN: *(Ritual greeting.)* Peace be to this house.

NIKOLAI & TANYA: *(Quickly, ritual response.)* With gladness we receive this peace, and with you joyfully praise it.

VERIGIN: God be praised.

TANYA: God be praised.

NIKOLAI: *(Calling.)* Mother! *(To them.)* God be praised.

VERIGIN: So you're the young man I've been hearing about.

NIKOLAI: I, what? Yes. I must be.

ANNA *appears in the doorway. Her sleeves are rolled up, her hands doughy, flour on her face.*

ANNA: Nikolai?

NIKOLAI: Mother, this is Peter Verigin.

ANNA: *(Not understanding.)* What?

NIKOLAI: Peter Verigin. *(To* VERIGIN.*)* This is my mother, Anna Ivanovna.

VERIGIN: A great pleasure.

ANNA, *in shock, just looks at him.*

TANYA: *(Covering, to* VERIGIN.*)* Are you hungry? We have plenty to eat.

VERIGIN: No, thank you—

TANYA: Something to drink?

VERIGIN: You know what I would love? A glass of water. I feel a bit...dusty.

TANYA: Of course.

She exits to the kitchen, past ANNA, *who suddenly kneels and bows, her forehead on the floor.*

NIKOLAI: Mother? Are you all right?

NIKOLAI *leans over* ANNA, *who grabs his arm, and pulls him down to his knees.* TANYA, *returning from the kitchen sees them, stops, watches.*

ANNA: *(Formally, with dignity.)* Peter Verigin. I welcome you with my heart. I salute you. Your coming is the coming of hope and joy. No more shall we be haunted by past suffering. I humbly put myself in your service.

She bows again to the floor. VERIGIN *looks at* NIKOLAI, *winks. Then he bows.* NIKOLAI *bows.*

VERIGIN: God be praised.

ANNA: God be praised.

NIKOLAI: *(Overlapping.)* God be praised.

VERIGIN: Please.

He holds out his hand, helps ANNA *to her feet.*

ANNA: *(As she stands.)* This is my son.

VERIGIN: Yes—

ANNA: Nikolai Savelyevitch. He's an important man. A leader.

NIKOLAI: Mother—

TANYA: Here we are.

TANYA *gives water to* VERIGIN.

VERIGIN: Thank you.

They watch him drink.

TANYA: The water is excellent here, in Canada.

VERIGIN: You don't find it slightly metallic?

TANYA: Metallic?

VERIGIN: I find that it tastes...bitter.

TANYA: I hadn't noticed.

NIKOLAI: I had. Yes, that's right. Slightly bitter.

TANYA *looks at* NIKOLAI.

VERIGIN: *(To* TANYA.*)* You have a beautiful home.

TANYA: Thank you.

VERIGIN: I like the little touches.

ANNA: We don't have much. We're good people.

VERIGIN: These candlesticks are beautiful. Are they silver?

NIKOLAI: Silver, yes.

VERIGIN: Beautiful. Did you inherit them?

TANYA: No.

VERIGIN: You bought them?

TANYA: Yes.

VERIGIN: *(Innocent.)* Really. With what?

TANYA: *(Slight pause.)* With money.

NIKOLAI: We sold a horse.

VERIGIN: Good for you. Tell me. Are all the people so prosperous?

TANYA: No, not everyone.

NIKOLAI: We're not exactly *prosperous*.

TANYA: Some of them refuse to work.

NIKOLAI: Yes, but that—

TANYA: You know what's good about this country?

VERIGIN: Tell me.

TANYA: If you work hard, you are rewarded. And there's no one to take it away.

VERIGIN *looks at* TANYA *a moment, then turns to* NIKOLAI.

VERIGIN: Do you have any children?

NIKOLAI: No. Not yet.

VERIGIN: I see.

Slight pause. Awkward.

ANNA: Nikolai was tortured in Russia.

NIKOLAI: Mother.

ANNA: He was, arrested and tortured. By the governor. He almost died.

NIKOLAI: We all suffered in Russia.

ANNA: We met your brother, Vasily Vasilyevitch. He came to our house, one night, I'll never forget. He showed us your letter, from Siberia. We were impressed.

NIKOLAI: Mother, *please*—

VERIGIN: My brother spoke very highly of you, Nikolai. Do you know what he called you?

NIKOLAI: No.

VERIGIN: He called you a man with a future.

ANNA: That's right.

VERIGIN: And not just my brother. Everyone I talk to, they're very impressed.

ANNA: A man with a future.

VERIGIN: I'm not trying to flatter you. I'm just telling you what I've heard. Because I don't know you. Yet. I don't know whether they're right. *(He smiles.)* I mean, who are you Nikolai? Hm? I can't wait to find out.

He pauses.

So. You've been to Ottawa.

NIKOLAI: Yes.

VERIGIN: Quite a journey. And you met with the Government.

NIKOLAI: That's right.

ANNA: Nikolai speaks fluent English.

VERIGIN: And you arranged for someone to come here. What was his name...?

NIKOLAI: Professor Mavor.

VERIGIN: Something about...registration?

NIKOLAI: It's just a formality. We have to sign for the land, to—

VERIGIN: *(Overlapping.)* To satisfy—

NIKOLAI: That's right, to satisfy their—

VERIGIN: Good. Good.

NIKOLAI: I was hoping I could speak with you—

VERIGIN: *(Interrupting.)* And you have done so?

NIKOLAI: Sorry?

VERIGIN: You have signed? Your name?

NIKOLAI: Yes. Myself and a couple of others.

TANYA: Most of the people refuse to sign. They're afraid. They don't understand.

NIKOLAI: This is why we need *you*, Peter Vasilyevitch. You will calm our fears. You will bring the light of understanding, into our darkness. You will make everything...smooth.

VERIGIN: Yes. Smooth.

Long pause. VERIGIN *looking at* NIKOLAI, *smiling slightly, thinking.*

VERIGIN: *(Breaking the moment. To* ANNA.) I'm afraid I must go.

ANNA: Already?

VERIGIN: It was a great pleasure meeting you. I can see that you have a noble spirit, a great strength, a *faith*. You love God, Anna. And I admire that. Very much.

ANNA *beams.*

Will you walk me to my carriage?

ANNA: Yes. Of course.

VERIGIN: All right then. Shall we?

He holds out his arm. ANNA *takes it. They move to the doorway. Just before he exits, he turns.*

(*To* NIKOLAI, *casual.*) I have a job for you, Nikolai. I'm setting up a committee. I'd like you to be on it. All right?

NIKOLAI: Yes.

VERIGIN: Good. You and Zibaroff.

NIKOLAI: *Ivan* Zibaroff?

VERIGIN: Is that a problem?

NIKOLAI *glances at* TANYA.

NIKOLAI: No, of course not.

VERIGIN: Good. We begin tomorrow night.

He exits, with ANNA. NIKOLAI *and* TANYA *stand, looking after them. Pause.*

ACT TWO—85

TANYA: So. That's him.

NIKOLAI: Yes. *(Slight pause.)* What.

TANYA: Nothing.

NIKOLAI: He's...I thought he'd be...taller.

TANYA *suddenly moves, puts away the linen and candlesticks.* NIKOLAI *watches her.*

What do you think the committee is for?

TANYA: I don't know.

NIKOLAI: I bet he wants to gather information. Start planning. You see what he's doing? He's pulling us together. What is it.

TANYA: Nothing.

NIKOLAI: Tanya.

TANYA: Nikolai. It's nothing.

Pause.

NIKOLAI: Well. I have work to do. Outside.

TANYA: Fine.

NIKOLAI: I won't be long.

TANYA *exits, into the kitchen. He stands, looking after her.*

Scene Six

The meeting room. NIKOLAI, VERIGIN, *and* ZIBAROFF. *They are in the middle of their meeting.*

ZIBAROFF: *(To* VERIGIN.*)* Where do they look for people to tax? In their book. Where do they look for soldiers? In their book. Where do they—

NIKOLAI: No, that's just not true.

ZIBAROFF: *(Pointing at* NIKOLAI.*)* His name is in this book. He put it there. He registered for land.

NIKOLAI: It doesn't mean I own it.

ZIBAROFF: No?

NIKOLAI: It still belongs to the village.

ZIBAROFF: No, it doesn't.

NIKOLAI: *(To* VERIGIN.*)* Look, there's something called the Hamlet Clause, it's part of the—

VERIGIN: *Does* it belong to the village?

NIKOLAI: Yes, it—

VERIGIN: Legally? Even though you signed for it?

NIKOLAI: All right, *technically*—

VERIGIN: What if you were to leave the village?

ZIBAROFF: That's right.

VERIGIN: What would happen to the land?

ZIBAROFF: It would go with him.

NIKOLAI: But, I wouldn't leave the village. That's the point.

VERIGIN: Really.

NIKOLAI: Yes, because I am loyal to *you*, Peter Vasilyevitch. I am a Doukhobor.

Slight pause.

They just need to fill in the blanks. It's paperwork. I don't even know what land I signed for, I couldn't tell you where it is. I just know that now, it belongs to the village.

VERIGIN: And how long would that last?

NIKOLAI: Forever. Look. The government wants to help us, it *likes* us. All it's saying is that this is a democracy, and, in order to be fair, to everyone else, we have to register our land. I promise you. It's nothing.

VERIGIN: You promise me.

NIKOLAI: Yes.

VERIGIN *places a document on the table.*

VERIGIN: Do you know what this is? It's the Homestead Act. I assume you've read it, Nikolai. After all, you speak with such authority. I assume that you know all about the oath.

NIKOLAI: The what?

VERIGIN: The oath of allegiance. To the King. Which, according to this, every man must swear within three years of signing his name. In the book. I assume that you are willing to swear this oath. And that confuses me.

NIKOLAI: Just a moment—

VERIGIN: Because, after all, as you've just told us: you're a Doukhobor.

Slight pause.

NIKOLAI: It doesn't apply to us.

VERIGIN: It doesn't?

ZIBAROFF: Hah!

NIKOLAI: It can't. They'll make a concession—

ZIBAROFF: Hah!

NIKOLAI: They, they are reasonable people—

ZIBAROFF: They are a government!

NIKOLAI: No—

ZIBAROFF: And we do not obey governments!

NIKOLAI: Listen—

ZIBAROFF: We obey God!

NIKOLAI: *(Shouts at* ZIBAROFF.*)* Stop it! I am talking! I am talking!

Pause.

VERIGIN: Do you know what I see when I look at you, Nikolai? I see a successful young man. A prosperous man. A man who has discovered wealth. And property. A man who is buying silver candlesticks, while all around him, his people, his brothers, go without. And I ask myself: what is this man capable of? To protect this wealth. This property. He is willing to make deals, with governments. Is he willing to fight? Is he willing to kill? What kind of person is he?

Pause.

What kind of person are you?

No response from NIKOLAI.

What kind of person are you?

ZIBAROFF *responds. It is the catechism.*

ZIBAROFF: I am a Doukhobor.

VERIGIN: Why are you called Doukhobor?

ZIBAROFF: To glorify God.

VERIGIN: What does the Doukhobor cross represent?

ZIBAROFF: A narrow path. Voluntary sorrow. A life of a pilgrim. A life of poverty.

VERIGIN: To what law do you belong?

ZIBAROFF: To God's law.

VERIGIN: What is God's law?

ZIBAROFF: What I do not wish for myself, I do not wish for my brother.

VERIGIN: Where do you see God?

ZIBAROFF: His sovereignty is everywhere.

VERIGIN: *(Looking at* NIKOLAI.) Ivan, would you do me a favour? I left some papers in my carriage. Would you fetch them please?

ZIBAROFF: Yes. Of course.

ZIBAROFF *exits.* VERIGIN *is gazing at* NIKOLAI.

NIKOLAI: Peter Vasilyevitch, I—

VERIGIN: No. Shh. Don't say anything. Come here, Nikolai.

Slight pause. Then, NIKOLAI *moves to him.*

Closer.

NIKOLAI *goes closer.*

You must listen, Nikolai. God is within you. Listen. What is He telling you? Listen. Listen.

NIKOLAI *bows his head, closes his eyes.* VERIGIN *watches him for a moment.*

Do you know what happened to me this morning? I was out walking. And I met a man, on the road. And he said to me, the man said: "Look." He pointed. "Look out there." And when I looked, I saw a vision. Rising up from the prairie. A community. Of people, of children. Working together, happy, singing. And I knew: there was no government there. No property. No laws except for one: Love God. And, as I looked, it seemed to me that from this vision, came a *light*, Nikolai, a golden light, spreading out in all directions, covering the prairie, moving out, across the world, the light of goodness, and of peace. The light of love. And when I turned again, the man was gone. And I just stood there, Nikolai...I stood there...bathed in golden light...and I felt...such...peace.

VERIGIN *puts a hand on* NIKOLAI'S *shoulder.* ZIBAROFF *has returned. He stands near the doorway, holding the papers, watching.*

Can you imagine such a place? Nikolai?

NIKOLAI: Yes.

VERIGIN: Can you?

NIKOLAI: *(Slight pause.)* Yes.

VERIGIN: Good. Because that is why you are here.

VERIGIN *waves* ZIBAROFF *over.* NIKOLAI *opens his eyes.*

Now. Our first step is: to build.

ZIBAROFF: Good.

VERIGIN: We work on the railroad until we have enough money to build a brick factory. Then, we use the bricks to build a sawmill.

ZIBAROFF: Ah hah.

VERIGIN: We buy machinery, for the fields, we increase productivity.

ZIBAROFF: Yes.

VERIGIN: All of it owned communally. We establish a central treasury which pays for everything and to which all profits are paid.

ZIBAROFF: I see.

VERIGIN: There will be three work periods in every day. A man will work five hours in the morning, have five hours rest, then work again in the evening. The next day, he only works the *middle* five hours, and so he *alternates*.

NIKOLAI: I have an idea.

VERIGIN: Yes?

NIKOLAI: We'll need some kind of headquarters, right? A village.

VERIGIN: Yes.

NIKOLAI: I know what to call it.

VERIGIN: What.

NIKOLAI: Verigin. The village...of Verigin.

Scene Seven

NIKOLAI *and* TANYA.

NIKOLAI: We have to make some changes.

TANYA: What do you mean.

NIKOLAI: We're giving away the horses.

TANYA: What?

NIKOLAI: All the animals. And all the tools. To the village.

TANYA: No we're not.

NIKOLAI: We're giving away the candlesticks.

TANYA: Nikolai—

NIKOLAI: We have too much. We're sinning.

TANYA: Who said—

NIKOLAI: My name is coming out of the book. I should never have signed in the first place.

TANYA: What? But—

NIKOLAI: *(Relentless.)* Verigin will sign. On behalf of the people.

TANYA: Verigin.

NIKOLAI: On every line. For every piece of land.

TANYA: That's ridiculous.

NIKOLAI: *(Exploding.)* WHAT DO YOU WANT? HOW ARE YOU A DOUKHOUBOR? IN WHAT WAY?

For a second, TANYA, *stunned, says nothing. Then she yells back.*

ACT TWO—93

TANYA: DON'T YELL AT ME!

Slight pause.

Do you want to know what I think? Are you interested? I think this is a bad idea. This community, it means that we will do the work, while Zibaroff goes around setting the animals free. I think Peter Verigin is a con. I think he wants us to suffer. He's doing us harm. How am I a Doukhobor? I have no idea, Nikolai, I really don't. I mean, are *you* a Doukhobor? Because you can do what Verigin tells you to do? Like a *puppet?* Because you can *suffer?*

She pauses.

I thought we left Russia behind. I thought this was going to be Canada.

Long pause. NIKOLAI *doesn't move. Then, finally, he speaks.*

NIKOLAI: *(Bleak.)* You're wrong. He doesn't want us to suffer. He just wants us to be....

TANYA: What.

NIKOLAI: Good. I have to believe that. I have to believe. I have to.

SCENE EIGHT

SIFTON'S *office, Ottawa.* JAMES McDOUGALL *sits behind the desk.* MAVOR *enters.*

MAVOR: Oh, I'm sorry. Have I got the wrong office?

McDOUGALL: No, no, please, come in. You're looking for the Minister?

MAVOR: Yes.

McDOUGALL: Professor James Mavor?

MAVOR: That's right, we have a meeting.

McDOUGALL: You do, yes.

MAVOR: Are you his assistant?

McDOUGALL: No, I'm not. You see, there's been a change.

MAVOR: A change?

McDOUGALL: Yes, I'm afraid the Minister's resigned.

MAVOR: What?

McDOUGALL: Yes, on Friday.

MAVOR: He resigned?

McDOUGALL: Yes, there's a new Minister now. Frank Oliver. I'm his assistant. *(Extending hand.)* James McDougall. It's a pleasure to meet you, Professor.

They shake.

MAVOR: I'm sorry, I'm...I wasn't informed about this.

McDOUGALL: Weren't you?

MAVOR: I'm rather surprised.

McDOUGALL: You're here about the Doukhobors?

MAVOR: That's right.

McDOUGALL: Yes. Mr. Oliver sends his regrets. Unfortunately he won't be able to be here today.

MAVOR: I see.

MCDOUGALL: However, he's asked me to take his place.

MAVOR: What?

MCDOUGALL: That's right. In fact, he's asked me to head up a special commission. To deal with the Doukhobor problem.

MAVOR: "Problem?"

MCDOUGALL: Yes. I'm looking forward to it. Quite a challenge. You see the Minister feels, and I agree, that the Doukhobors have been dealt with rather badly. Mr. Sifton was far too lenient. To the point, I'm afraid, of not even enforcing the laws. Of the country.

MAVOR: That's rubbish.

MCDOUGALL: I'm sorry?

MAVOR: I said, that's rubbish.

Pause.

MCDOUGALL: Well, I'll certainly pass that on. I'll make a note of your concern. I'm certain Mr. Oliver will take it under careful consideration.

MCDOUGALL *smiles pleasantly.*

However, in the meantime, the Minister feels, and I agree, that it's time to make some adjustments. In policy.

MAVOR: What kind of adjustments.

MCDOUGALL: *(Slight pause.)* Would you care to sit down?

Scene Nine

The prairie. Wind. NIKOLAI *stands, looks out.* ANNA's *voice is heard from off.*

ANNA: *(Off.)* Nikolai!

NIKOLAI *ignores her.*

(Off.) Nikolai!

ANNA *appears, in the background.*

Why are we stopped?

No response. She comes closer, but remains a distance from him.

You have a meeting.

NIKOLAI: I know.

ANNA: The government man has arrived. They're waiting for you.

NIKOLAI: I know.

ANNA: So why are we stopped? Let's go.

NIKOLAI: I don't want to.

ANNA: What do you mean?

NIKOLAI: I mean I don't want to.

ANNA: What is the matter with you?

No response.

Nikolai, come here.

No response.

Come here!

NIKOLAI *doesn't move.*

Well then. I'm going to walk. I'll tell them you broke a wheel, you'll be there in fifteen minutes. Nikolai? Fifteen minutes. *(Slight pause.)* Are you going to make me walk?

NIKOLAI *doesn't respond.* ANNA *exits, walking. Pause.* TANYA *appears, from the carriage.*

TANYA: What's happening. Where is she going.

NIKOLAI: She's walking.

TANYA: What? Why are we stopped?

NIKOLAI: I decided not to go to the meeting.

TANYA: Why not?

NIKOLAI *doesn't answer. He has heard something.*

Nikolai, what—

NIKOLAI: Sshh. Listen.

They listen. In the distance, carried unevenly on the wind, distant singing can be heard: a group of men's voices.

TANYA: Where are they.

NIKOLAI: I don't know. A long way away. It must be a work party. Coming home from the fields.

They listen. The singing fades to nothing. Wind.

TANYA: Is it because of me?

NIKOLAI: What.

TANYA: That you don't want to go.

NIKOLAI: No.

TANYA: I was wrong Nikolai. Okay? He didn't do us harm. And it's good that you're on the committee, and that he's going to sign for—

NIKOLAI: *(Interrupting.)* Are you happy?

TANYA: What?

NIKOLAI: Are you happy.

TANYA *just looks at him.*

NIKOLAI: Really? Because I'm not. I...

Pause. *He is suddenly on the verge of tears.*

I...

TANYA: What.

NIKOLAI: I can't find God anymore. Everywhere I look, He's...gone. I...I used to hear Him everywhere. His voice. When I was starving, and beaten, I never had any trouble then. He spoke to me, I could *hear* Him. But now...

Now, whenever I listen...I can't hear His voice. All I can hear is my own. And you know what it's doing?

TANYA: What.

NIKOLAI: Talking. It's talking.

Pause. TANYA *looking at him.*

TANYA: I hear God.

NIKOLAI: You do?

TANYA: Uh huh. All the time. I see Him too. I see Him when I look out there. I see Him when I look at you.

NIKOLAI *looks at her. Then he looks back out at the prairie.*

NIKOLAI: Do you know what this is?

TANYA: What.

NIKOLAI: *(Pointing to the prairie.)* This.

TANYA: It's the prairie.

NIKOLAI: Yes. But it's more than that.

TANYA: What do you mean.

NIKOLAI: It's...ours.

TANYA: What?

NIKOLAI: This is what I signed for. In the book.

TANYA: *(Slight pause.)* Really?

NIKOLAI: Yes.

Pause. They look.

TANYA: How much.

NIKOLAI: *(Pointing.)* See those trees? Out there?

TANYA: Yes.

NIKOLAI: Twice as far as that.

TANYA: Uh huh.

NIKOLAI: This way, almost to the slough.

TANYA: Uh huh.

NIKOLAI: And this way...as far as the dip.

They look.

> It hasn't even been broken yet. It might never be. Too far from the village.

TANYA: It's beautiful.

Pause.

> We shouldn't be doing this.

NIKOLAI: I know.

TANYA: We really shouldn't be doing this.

NIKOLAI: I know.

Pause. They look.

> Well.

TANYA: Yes.

NIKOLAI: I'm late for my meeting.

TANYA: I know.

NIKOLAI: All right. Let's go.

Pause. They don't move. They look out at the prairie.

Scene Ten

The meeting hall. McDOUGALL *sits at the table, with papers. Facing him:* VERIGIN *and* ZIBAROFF. *At the back of the hall, several Doukhobors, including* ANNA. *When they speak English,* NIKOLAI, ZIBAROFF, *and* VERIGIN *have thick accents. When they speak Russian, they have none. They have begun without* NIKOLAI. VERIGIN *is speaking, being very impressive, despite his terrible English.*

VERIGIN: Doukhobors wish to say: happy. Here we are: good citizens. Doukhobors. Teaching to Canada, teaching to Canada-people. Showing what is peace. What is *goodness*.

NIKOLAI *has entered.*

NIKOLAI: Where is the Professor?

They turn to him.

ZIBAROFF: *(Standing, to* McDOUGALL.*)* This is Kalmakoff, Nikolai.

McDOUGALL: Oh yes. Hello.

ZIBAROFF: *(To* NIKOLAI.*)* This is McDougall, James.

NIKOLAI: Where is Professor Mavor?

McDOUGALL: I'm afraid the Professor was unable to come. He sends his greetings, however, and his best wishes.

ZIBAROFF: Nikolai. Sit.

ZIBAROFF *pulls* NIKOLAI *into a chair.* VERIGIN *resumes.*

VERIGIN: As I say. Doukhobors are leaders. Lead the world...to peace. *(Russian word.)* Mir. Peace.

He pauses.

Because of this. I will write in book. For these lands. For every lands. Doukhobors who write already...*(He gestures to*

NIKOLAI.)...will remove. I will write. Thank you.

He sits. There is a pause.

McDOUGALL: Thank you, Mr. Verigin for your...generous offer. However. The Minister has instructed me to tell you that your previous agreement, with the previous Minister, is now void.

NIKOLAI: What?

McDOUGALL: If I may. *(He consults a document.)* You refuse to register vital statistics. You refuse to send your children to school. You refuse outright the Oath of Allegiance. And you refuse to cultivate more than 21.8 acres per quarter section of Doukhobor lands. This is unacceptable. Therefore, the Minister proposes the following changes.

NIKOLAI: Wait a minute—

McDOUGALL: First, all homesteads will be cancelled.

NIKOLAI: What?

McDOUGALL: Second, since we can't have eight thousand of you wandering homeless on the prairie, government-owned reserves, such as were created for the Indians, will be established around your villages. With an allowance of seventeen to twenty acres per person. These are the changes. However. *(He pauses.)* All those who take the Oath of Allegiance may keep their land. Provided they take up residence upon it, cultivate it, and provide the government with any and all information we deem pertinent.

NIKOLAI: But if we take up residence—

McDOUGALL: You must leave your villages. Yes. That is the offer.

VERIGIN: Doukhobors refuse.

NIKOLAI: *(To* McDOUGALL*)* Wait. Can we have a minute? To talk?

McDOUGALL: Of course.

NIKOLAI *speaks to* VERIGIN *and* ZIBAROFF *in Russian.* McDOUGALL *doesn't understand.*

NIKOLAI: *(To* VERIGIN.*)* He's bluffing. He's trying to provoke you, he's looking for a sign that you're willing to bend.

ZIBAROFF: He's trying to rob us.

NIKOLAI: *(Ignoring* ZIBAROFF, *focusing on* VERIGIN.*)* I promise you, they're willing to negotiate.

ZIBAROFF: You promise?

NIKOLAI: They want us to be Canadians. That's what this is—

ZIBAROFF: We are citizens of—

NIKOLAI: They are going to take our land!

VERIGIN: So? Let them take it. We will still be in Paradise.

NIKOLAI: What?

ZIBAROFF: That's right. Paradise.

VERIGIN: And they will be in Hell.

NIKOLAI: *(Pause.)* What?

VERIGIN: Does this surprise you, Nikolai? What did you expect him to say? This government man. *(Slight pause.)* Don't worry, Nikolai. I know exactly what to do.

ZIBAROFF: Listen to this.

VERIGIN: Have you ever heard of British Columbia?

ZIBAROFF: It's to the west.

VERIGIN: A wonderful place. The trees are laden with fruit.

ZIBAROFF: Luscious fruit, ready for picking.

VERIGIN: The sun is always shining there.

ZIBAROFF: There's mountains and rivers.

VERIGIN: A paradise. And best of all: No rules. No Homestead Act, no Oath of Allegiance.

ZIBAROFF: Only freedom.

NIKOLAI: Why are you telling me this.

VERIGIN: Because, my friend, we're going there.

NIKOLAI: Who is.

VERIGIN: We are. All of us. Imagine. A whole new community. Living together, working, in British Columbia. We will be happy there, Nikolai. We will live...in peace. *(Gestures to* McDOUGALL.*)* So, as far as I'm concerned, this meeting is over.

McDOUGALL: Finished?

VERIGIN: We cannot waste any more time. We have to start planning.

ZIBAROFF: That's right.

VERIGIN: I'm putting together a committee. I want you to be on it, Nikolai. All right? This evening at seven o'clock.

Pause. NIKOLAI *gazing at* VERIGIN.

NIKOLAI: *(English.)* Mr. McDougall.

McDOUGALL: Yes?

NIKOLAI: I wish to say. I despise what you have done.

McDOUGALL: I'm sorry?

NIKOLAI: You and your government. Have betrayed my people. Have broken your word.

McDOUGALL: Now just a moment—

NIKOLAI: *(His English breaking down.)* You promise us. We trust. We believe you are different. That this was good country.

VERIGIN: Yes.

NIKOLAI: That this was *Canada*.

ZIBAROFF: That's right.

VERIGIN: *(In Russian, to* NIKOLAI.*)* Well spoken, Nikolai.

NIKOLAI: *(Ignoring this.)* I do not like you. I do not trust you. However. I wish to take your oath.

VERIGIN: What?

NIKOLAI: *(To* McDOUGALL*)* Your oath of allegiance. Right now.

McDOUGALL: Well, I—

NIKOLAI: Right now!

McDOUGALL: *(Slight pause.)* All right. Just let me find the right form.

VERIGIN: *(In Russian.)* Nikolai. What are you doing?

NIKOLAI *looks at him.* ANNA *and* TANYA *are there.*

Do you know what you're doing? Listen inside yourself, Nikolai. What is He telling you?

McDOUGALL: Here we are.

VERIGIN: Nikolai.

McDOUGALL: Now. Put your hand on the Bible.

NIKOLAI *places his hand on the Bible.*

VERIGIN: Nikolai.

McDOUGALL: Repeat after me. I, Nikolai Kalmakoff.

VERIGIN: What is he saying?

McDOUGALL: I, Nikolai Kalmakoff.

NIKOLAI: I, Nikolai Savelyevitch Kalmakoff.

McDOUGALL: Do hereby swear allegiance.

NIKOLAI: Do hereby swear allegiance.

McDOUGALL: To my liege and lord, His Majesty, Edward the Seventh.

NIKOLAI: To my liege and lord, His Majesty, Edward the Seventh.

McDOUGALL: By the grace of God, King of England, and Lord of the British Empire.

NIKOLAI: By the grace of God, King of England, and Lord of the British Empire.

McDOUGALL: Duly sworn by me this day.

NIKOLAI: Duly sworn by me this day.

McDOUGALL: June the seventh, nineteen-oh-eight.

NIKOLAI: June the seventh, nineteen-oh-eight.

McDOUGALL: So help me God.

NIKOLAI: So help me God.

McDOUGALL: One moment.

He scribbles on a document.

Sign here.

NIKOLAI *signs.*

And here.

NIKOLAI *signs.*

And here.

NIKOLAI *signs.*

That's it. Welcome to Canada.

NIKOLAI *turns, locks eyes with* VERIGIN. *For a long moment, nothing. Then,* VERIGIN *sings the first line of a psalm. Several thousand Doukhobor voices sing the response.*

Scene Eleven

NIKOLAI *stands in the middle of the meeting room. The singing continues, grows in volume, until it is almost deafening. Several thousand Doukhobors cross the stage, singing, on the journey to* B.C. *They carry all their belongings on their backs. As they cross the stage, they pick up all the chairs and tables, and carry them away. They stream around* NIKOLAI, *who drops to his knees, and* TANYA, *who is still standing on the prairie. Then they recede. The singing dies away.*

Scene Twelve

NIKOLAI *and* TANYA *on the prairie.* NIKOLAI *is kneeling, head down. Wind.*

TANYA: Nikolai.

He looks up at her.

Come here.

He joins her.

NIKOLAI: Look at my hands.

TANYA: It's just soil. It'll wash off.

NIKOLAI: *(Staring at hands.)* You think so?

TANYA: Sshh.

They listen.

Do you hear that?

NIKOLAI: No. What?

TANYA: Listen.

They listen.

Just...listen.

As they stand there, the wind is gradually replaced by prairie sounds. A meadowlark sings. The sun comes out. They are bathed in golden evening sunlight. They listen. TANYA *holds out her hand.* NIKOLAI *takes it. They stand, looking out at the prairie, and listening.*

Lights fade.

THE END

Hristianovka Village, 1910, near Buchanan, Saskatchewan.

This large party—two wagons from each of 55 villages—passes through Yorkton enroute to Broadview, Saskatchewan, the railway embarkation point for the interior of British Columbia in 1909.

Frederick Edell as Nakashidze (L) and Tom Rooney as Nikolai.

(L-R) Tom Rooney as Nikolai, Sharon Bakker as Anna, and Kelly Handerek as Verigin.

PREMIERE PRODUCTION PHOTOS—III

(L-R) Sharon Bakker as Anna, Patricia Drake as Tanya, and Tom Rooney as Nikolai.

Tom Rooney as Nikolai and Patty Drake as Tanya.

ABOUT THE AUTHOR

GREG NELSON writes for both stage and radio. Stage plays that he has had produced include *Castrato, The Cure, Flight of the Living Dog, Sidney* and *Slow Zoom*. *Castrato* won Edmonton's Sterling Award for Best New Play, an Alberta Book Award, and first prize in the Canadian National Playwriting Competition. His adaptation of *Castrato* for CBC Radio's "Monday Night Playhouse" was nominated for a Gabriel Award.

Greg's other radio plays include *The Burning*, which is based on the Doukhobor material, *Johnny Colours, The Great Bakery Revolution*, and the one-hour radio comedy *Writing Butch*.

Born and raised in Central Canada, Greg received an MFA degree in Playwriting from the University of Alberta. A former playwright-in-residence at the University of Saskatchewan, he currently lives in Calgary.

PHOTO CREDITS

ACT I FRONTISPIECE: Courtesy Provincial Archives of British Columbia (92927).

PAGE 55, TOP: Courtesy Saskatchewan Archives Board (#S.B. 5447).

PAGE 55, BOTTOM: Courtesy Provincial Archives of British Columbia (47102).

ACT II FRONTISPIECE: Courtesy Provincial Archives of British Columbia *(detail)* (46932).

PAGE 58: Courtesy Provincial Archives of British Columbia (46932).

PAGE 109, TOP: Courtesy Provincial Archives of British Columbia (47194).

PAGE 55, BOTTOM: Courtesy Provincial Archives of British Columbia (46940).

PAGES 110-111: All courtesy Twenty Fifth Street Theatre, Saskatoon, Saskatchewan

Florence James Series

The Plainsman
by Ken Mitchell

Roundup
by Barbara Sapergia

Saskatoon Pie!
by Geoffrey Ursell

Talking Back
by Don Kerr

Eureka! Seven One-Act Plays for Secondary Schools
edited by Jacquie Johnston Lewis and Dianne Warren

Club Chernobyl
by Dianne Warren

Z: A Meditation on Oppression, Desire and Freedom
by Anne Szumigalski

Some Assembly Required
by Eugene Stickland

Spirit Wrestler
by Greg Nelson